For all of the emphasis that ʃ of our nation and politics, wha formation. The real enemy is see. I challenge you to read t. strategies your enemy uses against you.

MIKE HUCKABEE
Former Arkansas Governor
Republican Candidate for President
Former Fox News host

You wish to learn the tactics of our enemy, the devil? Learn from one that has a different approach due to his background in intelligence. It's time to take back what has been stolen.

JOHNNY HUNT
Senior Pastor, First Baptist Church Woodstock
Past President, Southern Baptist Convention

As a former SWAT team member and police officer, Pastor Phil Hopper brings an invaluable perspective to understanding the devices and strategies employed by our true adversary. While *Defeating the Enemy* is a scholarly and theological study, it's also a practical how-to guide. Regardless of your background and experience, this book will equip you to live a life of victory, because as the Scriptures remind us, we are more than conquerors in Christ.

REV. SAMUEL RODRIGUEZ
President of the National Hispanic
Christian Leadership Conference

As Christians, we are all involved in a conflict in the realm of the spirit. Unfortunately, entire segments of the Body of Christ refuse to acknowledge that they have a sinister and insidious adversary whose purpose is to steal from them, kill them, or destroy them by any means available to him. Pastor Phil Hopper has used his training as a police officer and SWAT team member to gain valuable insights into the subject of spiritual warfare. I encourage every believer to read this book wherein Pastor Phil will outline strategies on how to recognize your enemy, understand his methods of operation, and prevail against him every time.

DR. ROD PARSLEY
Pastor and Founder, World Harvest Church
Columbus, Ohio

Defeating the Enemy is a winning playbook for life. Building a championship culture in your family requires you to anticipate the moves of your opponent, the devil himself, and counter in a way that gives you the victory. Phil is a man of unparalleled integrity and knowledge of Scripture. This book is a home run!

DAYTON MOORE
General Manager, Kansas City Royals

Phil is a leader in the best of ways. He is humble, transparent, and firm in his beliefs. In today's world of leaders saying mostly what is safe and non-offensive, *Defeating the Enemy* is presented with a direct, biblically-based message about what Jesus has done *for* and expects *from* Christians and how Satan distorts and interferes both obviously and insidiously. Prepare yourself to be educated, challenged, uncomfortable, and enlightened.

RYAN LEFEBVRE
Radio and Television Announcer
Kansas City Royals

As my pastor and friend, Phil Hopper has always led with integrity and honor, keeping God's truth at the forefront. With *Defeating the Enemy*, his first published book, he helps us discover God's battle plan for victory over an ever-present evil, how to break the chains of captivity, and live the abundant life we are called to live. An AMAZING book every person should read!

LES NORMAN
Former Kansas City Royals
Media Personality

From college athlete to SWAT officer to pastor—talk about seeing and experiencing it all! Pastor Phil Hopper not only puts his heart and soul into his church ministry, he also walks with a passion for revealing the truth in a wayward world. *Defeating the Enemy* is true enlightenment on the real enemy and powers we fight in our earthly lives. Winning, although it can be reflected on a scoreboard, can be achieved in our daily lives, especially when we recognize the opponent. Pastor Phil has provided an outstanding avenue for understanding and ultimate victory!

DANAN HUGHES
Former Wide Receiver, Kansas City Chiefs
Analyst Big Ten Network

Although the title is *Defeating the Enemy*, it could as easily be called *Conquering with Christ*. Certainly, you're exposed to the devices used by the enemy, but more importantly, you're reminded of the supreme sacrifices made by our Savior that assures our victory over sin. You'll fall in love with Jesus all over again as

Hopper shares with you how you can live the abundant life.

TERENCE CHATMON
President & CEO, Do Your Children Believe, Inc.
CEO, Fellowship of Companies for Christ

During my 16-year MLB career, I always wanted to know my opponent's game plan! How they were going to pitch me, how they were going to defend me and how they were going to attack me. Many times before the first pitch of the game was thrown, I knew victory was inevitable because I knew their game plan!

Pastor Phil Hopper brilliantly unveils our enemy's game plan which will help us live with peace and freedom in the abundant life that Jesus offers to us all. Pastor Phil gives us the enemy's playbook so victory is our only option!

MIKE SWEENEY
Five-time MLB All-Star
Kansas City Royals Hall of Fame

DEFEATING
THE
ENEMY

DEFEATING

THE

ENEMY

EXPOSING AND OVERCOMING
THE STRATEGIES OF SATAN

PHIL HOPPER

DESTINY IMAGE® PUBLISHERS, INC.

P.O. Box 310, Shippensburg, PA 17257-0310

"Promoting Inspired Lives."

This book and all other Destiny Image and Destiny Image Fiction books are available at Christian bookstores and distributors worldwide.

Cover design by Eileen Rockwell
Interior design by Terry Clifton

For more information on foreign distributors, call 717-532-3040.

Reach us on the Internet: www.destinyimage.com.

ISBN 13 TP: 978-0-7684-1782-1
ISBN 13 eBook: 978-0-7684-1783-8
ISBN 13 HC: 978-0-7684-1785-2
ISBN 13 LP: 978-0-7684-1784-5

For Worldwide Distribution, Printed in the U.S.A.
1 2 3 4 5 6 7 8 / 22 21 20 19 18

I dedicate this book to the most precious people in my life: Christa, Jake, Makay and Josh. You are the greatest blessing I have this side of heaven.

ACKNOWLEDGMENTS

Nobody accomplishes anything of significance alone. And this book is the culmination of the contribution of multiple amazing people.

To Lisa Deacy, my Executive Assistant, thank you for the hours spent transcribing, typing, editing and reading. You are a blessing to my life.

To Debbie Stiegler, God sent you to us at precisely the right time. I am so thankful for you.

To my amazing staff and congregation at Abundant Life: It is such an honor to be your pastor. I love you all.

CONTENTS

FOREWORD

When a 6'6" man walked into my office one day, need-less to say, his frame immediately caught my attention. As this zealous and teachable leader entered my life, I was intrigued with his story.

From law enforcement and active service in the SWAT team of Kansas City to the gospel ministry and leading a church, Phil Hopper is a new man changed by the power of God. Phil and his church are a living testimony of God's miracu-lous power in today's world.

Phil Hopper has learned how to win in his life. Through his life in law enforce-ment, God has prepared him with a unique perspective of winning in life spiritually. What you hold in your hand is a book on how to win in your life spiritually.

Defeating the Enemy is the only way to win in life, not just spiritually, but holistically. We are in a war, and our war is not against people and countries, but against our greatest enemy alive, Satan himself.

From a snowy night on an interstate when he almost lost his life to where he is today, his is a life story about defeating the enemy of his life and ours. While this world tells you that you cannot win in life, God's message is completely different. What God has done and is doing in and through the life and leadership of Phil Hopper, God can do for you.

With his expertise in law enforcement, Phil Hopper conducts Christian espionage on this common enemy of all mankind, systems, structures, and countries. Sharing biblical and practical insights he has learned and lived out, he will teach you how to win by defeating your enemy.

Thousands of people hear this man speak each weekend. I believe that thousands will read this book and share it with friends across the world.

Phil Hopper is a giant! Not just physically, but even more so spiritually. He is not perfect, but he is progressing each day into becoming more of what God wants him to be.

This is possible only because he has learned how to win in his life. I hope and pray that you will let him instruct you and inspire you to win also. Winning is not determined by your physique and charisma. Winning the daily battle with Satan is determined by persevering through all that you face in life and committing yourself to living God's way.

Defeating the Enemy will teach you how to win God's way.

DR. RONNIE FLOYD
Senior Pastor, Cross Church
Past President, Southern Baptist Convention

WHO DOESN'T LIKE A GOOD SPY MOVIE?

I most certainly do! Give me some "James Bond 007" or "Mission Impossible" with Tom Cruise or the "Jason Bourne" series starring Matt Damon. They are box-office hits for a reason. They are exciting stories of espionage, with lots of danger in the age-old struggle between good and evil.

The truth is I have done far more than just sit on the couch watching reruns of old movies. I am living it every day, and whether you realize it or not, you are too.

Before becoming a pastor, I spent eight years on the streets of Kansas City, Missouri, in law enforcement. Several of those years were spent on the Kansas City SWAT team. I always wanted to go undercover, but with a 6' 6" frame, I had a difficult time blending in. My physique lent itself more naturally to picking up a battering ram and breaking through doors where the bad guys lived. But without the undercover agents first doing the *"intelligence gathering,"* those of us on the SWAT side would have never known where to go. The best part of the job was setting up our "surveillance"—watching and learning the moves of the bad guys without them knowing they were being watched, and then when they least expected it, making ours.

You might be thinking it is a pretty unusual résumé for the pastor of a church, but in many ways, it gives me a level of insight that no seminary training ever could. The time spent as a cop on the streets of Kansas City and specifically in SWAT training equipped me in ways for the ministry unlike any PhD in theology. People have often asked me why I wanted to go into law enforcement. I first give them the interview answer that, "I wanted to help people," and then I tell them the real answer, "I didn't want to be bored." Indeed, for eight years as a member of the Kansas City Police Department, I never once was bored. In fact, there were many moments that were very intense. Winston Churchill, who fought in World War I, once said, "Nothing is more exhilarating than being shot at and missed." To that, I say, "Amen!"

What I couldn't have imagined then was that God was actually preparing me in a very unique way for an even greater mission. It is the same mission we all share as followers of Jesus—to advance a Kingdom and bring glory to the King. Even then as a member of the police force, I realized the parallels between engaging a flesh and blood enemy that is trying to take you out and an unseen enemy that is equally committed to your complete destruction. And, I realized the necessity of understanding the enemy—both seen and unseen—through espionage and intelligence gathering.

In this book, I'm going to share with you a lot of what I've learned, and together we're going to do some Christian intelligence on the adversary—that old serpent, the devil. The Apostle Paul said in Second Corinthians 2:11 that we "are not ignorant of his [Satan's] devices." Yet so many Christians today are just that. Satan has stolen so much ground from them so many times, and it's time to take back that stolen territory. The devil is incredibly intelligent and extremely wicked, but our warfare with him is entirely winnable because he is also completely predictable. As you are about to discover, because we know how he operates, we can learn how to not only overcome the attacks of the enemy but ultimately avoid them altogether.

A number of years ago, I had the exciting privilege of traveling to the Mediterranean and retracing some of the Apostle Paul's footsteps. I stood on Mars Hill in Athens. I walked the ancient streets of Corinth and stood in front of the Bema Seat—where Paul himself would have stood to address the people. The real highlight of the trip was touring the age-old city of Ephesus, one of the most influential cities of the ancient world. It is where the Apostle Paul planted the early Christian church of Ephesus—one of the seven churches spoken of in the Book of Revelation.

As we were touring the ruins of the very places where Paul would have been, our tour guide stopped to show us a carving etched in the stone paving on one of the streets of Ephesus by one of the very early Christians. It was the same fish symbol that many Christians drive around with today on the back of their car. (If you're one of them, please refrain from road rage!) It was a secret symbol of early Christianity that would let other Christians entering the city know there was a Christian community nearby.

Those were the days before they could post a church sign on a building to let people know when and where they were meeting. Like many places in the world even today, these early Christians lived in places where fol- lowing Jesus could get you killed. Satan attempted for generations to destroy the Church through persecution. What he failed to do through persecution, he has sadly accomplished over and over again through infiltration and deception.

As I was listening to the tour guide explain the fish symbol, it hit me—as these early Christians were try- ing to survive the onslaught of persecution from an enemy they could see, the Apostle Paul was providing key intelligence about the enemy they could not see. Their real persecutors were not the Romans they could see. Our real enemy is always the one we can't see—the spiritual power pulling the strings behind the scenes. In Ephesians chapter 6, Paul provided every Christian with a strategic field manual for conducting spiritual warfare.

> *Finally, my brethren, be strong in the Lord and in the power of His might. Put on the whole armor of God, that you may be able to stand against the wiles of the devil. For we do not wrestle against flesh and blood, but against principalities, against powers, against the rulers of the darkness of this age, against spiritual hosts of wickedness in the heavenly places. Therefore take up the whole armor of God, that you may be able to withstand in the evil day, and having done all, to stand. Stand therefore, having girded your waist with truth, having put on the breastplate of righteousness, and having shod your feet with the preparation of the gospel of peace; above all, taking the shield of faith with which you will be able to quench all the fiery darts of the wicked one. And take the helmet of salvation, and the sword of the Spirit, which is the word of God.*
>
> —EPHESIANS 6:10-17

The early Christians found themselves at war with the adversary of our soul—the devil himself. It is the battle of the ages that continues to this day; and it is raging around us all the time. The battle lines were drawn when Jesus announced in John 10:10, "The thief does not come except to steal, and to kill, and to destroy. I have come that they may have life, and that they may have it more abundantly."

The average Christian lives in captivity, even though Jesus came to give us abundant life. Through the pages of this book, I want to help you overcome those areas of your life that have hindered you from living the abundant life in Christ, show you how to stay free once you are free, and ultimately help you avoid falling captive to the devil's devious tactics in the first place.

Everything God wants to give us, Satan wants to steal from us. While his tactics have never changed, in 21st-century America, he has been emboldened by the wickedness of our times and the vast array of enticements at his disposal to lure us into captivity. We have been given a weapon far greater than any hell can devise: the power of God. And when God is for us, who can be against us? I have read the end of the book, and we win! But that does not mean there will not be a fight to the finish.

Many people simply do not believe in the reality of Satan. You may be among them, and I hope to change your mind because he is probably at work in your life right now. Maybe you think he is a figment of somebody's imagination, or perhaps you are like millions who think he is simply a symbol of evil. I'm not asking you to take my word for it. Jesus spent 40 days in the wilderness with him, and He testifies over and over that Satan is a real person. If you want to be victorious over his attacks, you better be ready when he comes calling in your home, your life, or your family.

Whether you realize it or want to admit it, you are an enemy of the devil and he is an enemy of you. As Christians, we are at war with a very real enemy with a highly organized army of fallen angels. Second only to Almighty God, he is the most powerful being in the universe. The Hebrews call him Satan, and the Greeks call him the devil. His armies of fallen angels are the very ones Paul talks about in Ephesians 6:12.

When did this war begin?

Why are we at war?

What is it exactly that Satan wants?

In the pages that follow, I not only answer these questions, but I will provide you with a firm foundation of knowledge about your sworn enemy. If you lack the knowledge of God, you will lack the power of God. For that reason, this book is both deeply theological and highly practical. Only when you become equipped with this knowledge—the strategic intel on your adversary— can you fully understand what Paul was expressing to the Christians at Ephesus.

One of the core problems in today's culture is there are many Christians who have never grown up spiritually. In Ephesians 4:14, Paul said, "We should no longer be children, tossed to and fro and carried about with every wind of doctrine." Children are easily deceived and thus easy prey for the adversary. God wants you to grow up to spiritual maturity so you can live in victory.

If all you ever do is live on the milk of God's Word, ultimately you are going to remain a toddler your entire spiritual life. So we are going to do a little espionage to give you some real meat in your spiritual diet. Get ready to do some deep digging.

Just as the U.S. Government's Central Intelligence Agency conducts espionage on our nation's enemies, as Christians it is imperative we conduct some intelligence gathering on ours. We need to dig into our adversary's past, find out who he is, what he does, and what exactly he wants. Let us begin our espionage by taking a journey back through time to the beginning so we can discover how this battle began and the motivation behind Satan's devotion to his relentless reign of destruction.

Let's begin and let's prepare to win.

PART I

THE BATTLE
OF THE AGES

CHAPTER 1

ROUND ONE: BACK TO THE BEGINNING

If we really want to discover how this epic battle between God and the devil began—and why it is still raging today—we have to go back to the beginning, even before the creation of Adam.

Ezekiel 28 provides the earliest record we have of the one we now know as Satan. It gives us a telling description of him even before he ever emerges as the serpent in Genesis 3.

> *Moreover the word of the Lord came to me, saying, "Son of man, take up a lamentation for the king of Tyre, and say to him, 'Thus says the*

Lord God: You were the seal of perfection, full of
wisdom and perfect in beauty.'"
—EZEKIEL 28:11-12

Part of spiritual maturity is learning to look beyond the physical to see the spiritual. You have physical eyes, but you need to develop spiritual eyes because there is always more going on than what immediately "meets the eye."

Walking through the mall recently with my wife, I encountered a display of artwork for sale—digitally made pictures full of nothing but randomly colored dots. I asked the salesclerk what they were, and she informed me they were "stereograms"—beautiful, intricate scenes embedded in an array of dots. All I could see were the randomly colored dots. I began to argue with her. "No way," I said. "All I see are dots!" She assured me if I looked at them long enough, I would eventually see an amazing 3D scene. So I stared...and nothing emerged. I stared some more; still nothing. Then my wife saw the picture. Others around me could see it. But me? Just dots. Then I became determined! We were not leaving the mall until I saw the 3D scene. I stared and stared and stared some more, and then it happened. A picture began to pop off the canvas. I could finally see the real scene that did not "immediately meet the eye."

Much of Scripture is like that. This lamentation or proverb in Ezekiel 28 is not merely directed at the physical king—what immediately meets the eye. In the physical realm, this passage is talking about the physical

King of Tyre who was an earthly, wicked king. But he cannot be the real emphasis in this passage. No, there must be another, because the King of Tyre was never the "seal of perfection."

Keep reading because there is more than meets the eye. Much more! As you are about to see, in reality, this passage is directed to the spiritual king pulling the strings of the physical king—the same spiritual king who was pulling Peter's strings in Matthew 16:23.

Right before Jesus went down to Jerusalem, He announced to His disciples He was going to the cross and He was going to die. Immediately Peter began to rebuke Him saying, "Jesus, you can't do that, you are the Messiah, you are the King, and you are not going to the cross." Jesus looked right at Peter and said, "Get behind Me, Satan." Why? Jesus could see beyond the physical person to the spiritual power pulling Peter's strings.

If you do not want to be a puppet on a string, you need to put everything under the light of Scripture. There is always more going on than meets the eye. Your real enemy is not your ex-spouse. (I promise it was not a pitchfork he was holding the other day, just a garden rake!) Your boss isn't either. (Even if you swore you saw 666 tattooed on his forehead.) It's not your neighbor, your coworker, or any other enemy you can see. Your real adversary is the one you can't see.

In fact, most of the people in our lives who attack us or attempt to hurt us are nothing more than puppets at the mercy of a puppet master. They are Satan's little prisoners. Sadly, they are the worst kind of prisoners—prisoners unaware! Once you can see past the physical, it becomes easy to avoid getting caught in Satan's snare. You'll find that God will give you wisdom and a tempered response to counter every advance of the adversary.

Ezekiel 28:13 confirms this passage has nothing to do with a physical person because the King of Tyre had never been in the Garden of Eden. Long before Adam's creation, there was another of God's creations in the Garden known as the "anointed cherub." The earth was his home and the Garden was his throne.

> *You were in Eden, the garden of God; every precious stone was your covering: the sardius, topaz, and diamond, beryl, onyx, and jasper, sapphire, turquoise, and emerald with gold. The workmanship of your timbrels and pipes was prepared for you on the day you were created.*
> —Ezekiel 28:13

As we walk back in time (we don't know really how long ago) in our intelligence gathering on the adversary, we discover Lucifer used to be a beautiful, absolutely unique, very special, and magnificent creation of God. He was the crowning jewel of the entire angelic host, full of wisdom, perfect in beauty, absolutely beyond imagination. Lucifer was not just decked out in a lot of bling. He did not have a big gold medallion hanging around his neck with his shirt unbuttoned. His very being was made of jewels and gemstones. The very name Lucifer means light bearer or shining one.

Lucifer was created to not only bear the light of God but to reflect it as well because God is light. First John 1:5 says, "In Him is no darkness at all." Every time God shows up in the Bible in all of His unveiled glory, it is in a blaze of light so brilliant it is blinding to look upon. When Jesus made an appearance on the road to Damascus in Acts 9, Saul was instantly blinded by the brilliant, blazing white light of the Son of God.

Take just a moment to let this sink in. Here is this very special creation of God whose body, the essence of his being, is glowing and glistening with the most exquisite jewels and gemstones. The blinding brilliance of God passes through this incredible being standing before His throne, exploding on the other side. Suddenly the universe is flooded with this brilliant rainbow of light.

God didn't stop there. Lucifer is not only made of jewels and gemstones, but Ezekiel 28:13 tells us he was made of timbrels (tambourines) and pipes like you would find in a pipe organ. Lucifer does not simply *have* musical instruments at his disposal; his entire being *is* a musical instrument.

Job 38:7 provides us with a clue as to why God created Lucifer with musical instruments as a part of his being. It tells us as God laid the foundations of the earth and everything in it, the morning stars—the angelic race God created long before the Adamic race—sang together and shouted for joy. Lucifer was created to be the worship leader of the entire angelic host, leading the praise and worship of God. That was his commission.

Do you ever wonder why so much of the time in churches worship becomes more like WAR-ship, with church members going to war over their "style" of worship—as if the worship belongs to them and not God? Somebody once said when Lucifer was cast out of heaven, he landed right smack dab in the middle of the choir loft of the nearest church. My personal observation, after years and years in the church, is there is probably a lot more truth to that than most of us can imagine. As the one who used to lead other beings in the worship of God, his desire is now to steal the worship from God. He wants it, and more than anything, he does not want God to get it.

Lucifer would lead multiplied legions of angels to love, worship, praise, and exalt God. And he carried out his mission not in heaven, but on earth in the Garden of Eden (see Ezek. 28:13).

This incredible being was made to radiate and reflect the light of God throughout the entire universe. He was placed by God on planet earth in the beautiful garden called Eden. From there, he would lead the other morning stars in the praise and worship of God. As the anointed cherub, God had given him dominion over the earth.

You were the anointed cherub who covers; I established you; you were on the holy mountain of

God; you walked back and forth in the midst of
the fiery stones.

—EZEKIEL 28:14

The word "anointed" in verse 14 is the same word in the Hebrew as "messiah." Just as Jesus is called the Messiah, Lucifer was the "messianic cherub." Messiah is a title that means "anointed one" and implies authority and supremacy. Don't be confused by that. Lucifer has never been Christ's equal. Unlike Lucifer, Jesus is deity. He has existed for all of eternity as the second Person of the Trinity. He is the one who created all that is—including Lucifer (see Col. 1:16). Lucifer is called the "messianic" cherub because he had been given dominion and authority over the earth. As the "anointed cherub," God gave him a throne in Eden where he ruled as king over God's earthly kingdom made up of the angelic host.

Lucifer was not created as an adversary. This isn't the yin and yang of Eastern mysticism—the George Lucas theology of Star Wars—"The Force." The anointed cherub was created perfectly, and he was created holy.

You were perfect in your ways from the day you
were created, till iniquity was found in you.
By the abundance of your trading [all those
musical instruments] *you became filled with*
violence within, and you sinned; therefore I cast
you as a profane thing out of the mountain of
God; and I destroyed you, O covering cherub,

from the midst of the fiery stones. Your heart was
lifted up because of your beauty.
—EZEKIEL 28:15-17

We do not know a lot about what was going on at that time on the earth when Lucifer reigned from Eden. Scripture does record there came a day when this being known as Lucifer challenged God to war. Today we are finding ourselves squarely in the midst of this warfare. It is a war for the world, a battle for a kingdom, and a struggle that began in the Garden of Eden. It is the same war that Paul alludes to in Ephesians 6:12 when he says, "We do not wrestle against flesh and blood, but against principalities, against powers, against the rulers of the darkness of this age, against spiritual hosts of wickedness in the heavenly places."

It is a battle for a kingdom—
Lucifer coveted God's crown
and he coveted God's throne.

Here is the reality. Lucifer was lifted up because there came a day when he thought to himself, "You know, I am a very special creation, yes I am." And he began to be lifted up with pride. He thought to himself, "I am so good lookin'—I could be Mr. Universe." He began to look at himself with all those stones and gems—the sapphires, turquoise, and emeralds. He began to say, "You know, I really am beautiful…I am like the King of Bling! There is nobody else in this universe quite like me. Nobody else has these jewels and these instruments." Suddenly, he realized all the morning stars were focused on him when they were worshiping God. And then it happened. He became so lifted up in pride, he wanted to be worshiped as God. He wanted to sit on the throne of God, and he wanted to steal the Kingdom of God.

Isaiah 14:12-14 provides more key intel about the motivation of Lucifer's insidious revolt that rocked the world.

> *"How you are fallen from heaven, O Lucifer, son of the morning! How you are cut down to the ground, you who weakened the nations! For you have said in your heart: 'I will ascend into heaven, I will exalt my throne above the stars of God; I will also sit on the mount of the congregation on the farthest sides of the north; I will ascend above the heights of the clouds, I will be like the Most High.'"*

This puffed-up peacock called Lucifer had an "I" problem, a lot like you and me sometimes. Five times he says, "I." He said, "I will ascend into heaven." Why did he have to ascend into heaven? Don't miss this—Lucifer was not in heaven when the insurrection started. Where was he? He was here on the earth. He looked up there, and he didn't want his throne down here. He said, "I will ascend into heaven" because he wanted that throne up there. No longer satisfied with his throne in Eden, his heart was consumed with lust for the throne of God in heaven.

The same pride of life that consumed Lucifer was Eve's downfall (more about that later) and litters our history books with names like Nebuchadnezzar, Julius Caesar, Hitler, and Stalin. You realize it's the same syndrome that has perhaps plagued your boss at one time or another who wasn't into "team building"—arrogant and closed to any kind of feedback. I know plenty of moms struggle with this same syndrome. It comes out in the desire to keep up with little Suzy or Johnny's overachiever mom. She's the one bringing over-the-top refreshments to the school party or football or soccer practice. Birthday parties are never just a happy gathering of her child's friends—they're an event of outlandish proportions.

Pride is a destroyer of relationships. It hinders our ability to reach our potential and distorts our perspective on reality. Arrogance opens the door to taking shortcuts that compromise our values. Just consider the wreckage in the wake of Lucifer's prideful rebellion. Revelation 12:4 tells us he took a third of the angels with him that rebelled against God. With that army of fallen angels, he waged war against God because he wanted to be worshiped as God. All of creation is still reeling from his rebellion and the mind-numbing destruction driven by his inflated ego.

You defiled your sanctuaries by the multitude of your iniquities, by the iniquity of your trading [the musical instruments, the jewels]; therefore I brought fire from your midst; it devoured you, and I turned you to ashes upon the earth in the sight of all who saw you."

—EZEKIEL 28:18

I want you to see something that is very important here. Lucifer lost his position as the anointed cherub, and he was cast out of the third heaven—the same place that Paul spoke of in Second Corinthians 12:2 when he said he had been caught up to the "third heaven."

The Bible teaches there are three heavens which are somewhat outlined for us in Psalm 148. The earth and its atmosphere are the first heaven, what we know as outer space is the second heaven, and the dwelling place of God is the third heaven. Lucifer waged war in the third heaven. In Luke 10:18, Jesus tells us how He "saw Satan fall like lightening from heaven" as he was cast out of the third heaven into the second heaven.

It is important to understand Satan's headquarters, where he assaults the earth, is not in hell. You see pictures of Satan with red pajamas and a pitchfork with little horns on his head and fire all around him. That is not what he looks like, and the fiery pit of hell is not his dwelling place.

The day is coming when hell will most certainly be Satan's eternal home, and he will forever be bound in the lake of fire. But he does not reign there. Ephesians

2:2 calls him "the prince of the power of the air." Ephesians 6:12 says that "rulers of the darkness" are the spiritual rulers over the world, and "spiritual hosts of wickedness in the heavenly places." The phrase "heavenly places" is not a reference to heaven (as in the dwelling place of God). It is a reference to the "heavens" as in outer space. The second heaven is described in Psalm 148:3-4 as the sun, the moon, and the stars. It is the second heaven that Paul is referring to as "heavenly places," and it is from there Satan plans his assault upon the earth.

Satan lost his position as the anointed cherub. No longer could he reign over the earth—he had been cast out of heaven. He had nowhere to land for he no longer had a throne upon the earth. He lost his name. No longer is he known as Lucifer; he became Satan, "the accuser." He is the one Jesus called the "Prince of Darkness," he is the one Paul called in Ephesians 6:12 the "ruler of darkness." Have you ever wondered where the "darkness" came from in Genesis 1:2 if indeed "God is light and in Him is no darkness at all" (1 John 1:5)? The rebellion of the "light bearer" took place between Genesis 1:1 and 1:2, and God judged the light bearer's sin with darkness.

No longer the light bearer, Satan has become the prince of darkness. Do not think for one moment that the prince of darkness does not still transform himself into an "angel of light" today (2 Cor. 11:14). In our society, his #1 tactic is not to be the roaring lion of intimidation but rather a deceptive angel of light through infiltration. I'll share much more about that later.

Some cultures around the world, especially in tribal areas, are taken captive through fear of the "spirits." They worship the "gods" out of fear and only hope to appease them. As the "roaring lion," Satan seeks to control through fear and intimidation. But in America, he wants to infiltrate our lives without being noticed. His methods in western society include less fear and intimidation and more deception and infiltration. He uses other people who are his unwitting prisoners and puppets. It may be your boss or coworker of the opposite sex that is so easy to talk to. It is easy to be fooled, but with God's help, you are going to learn—just like I learned as a member of the SWAT team—to immediately discern the enemy's strategy *before* he begins to wreak havoc.

God's plan has been to establish an earthly kingdom that will be without end, and we would be His sons and daughters. In this great cosmic clash—it does not matter when, it does not matter how—God has never been on the ropes. He has never been taken by surprise by Satan. God knew exactly what was going to happen, and he knew exactly what He was going to do. He will never leave you without a way of escape or without hope. He has had a very specific plan for your life before you were ever born, and He has provided all the tools and weapons you will ever need to live victoriously and to become sharp and discerning to the tactics of the adversary.

CHAPTER 2

ROUND TWO: THE GARDEN OF EDEN

Round Two of this cosmic conflict opens in the same venue where Lucifer once reigned and ruled: the Garden of Eden. It is here that God was about to do something that had never been done before. He announced His intention in Genesis 1:26, "Let Us make man in Our image, according to Our likeness; let them have dominion over…the earth."

Satan and all the fallen angels we know today as demons heard what God said. And they knew exactly what it meant. This very special creation would have what Satan had always wanted—the image and likeness of God. If you ever want to know what God is like, all you have to do is look at how God created man.

God is a triune being—Father, Son, and Holy Spirit—one God eternally existing in three Persons. So God did what He said He would do. He created man as a triune being—with a spirit, soul, and body. Genesis 2:7, "And the Lord God formed man of the dust of the ground"—that is your body; and "breathed into his nostrils the breath of life"—your spirit; "and man became a living being"—your soul (your conscience, mind, will, and emotions). Just as God is three in one, He made man three in one. When God did what He said He would do—make man in His image—Satan was consumed with jealousy.

In Isaiah 14:14, you can almost hear him seething with jealous rage when he announces, "I will be like the Most High," but he wasn't like the Most High. Satan immediately hated Adam because Adam had what he always wanted—to be like God. To make matters even worse, Adam had what Satan used to have. God not only made Adam like Him, He also gave him "dominion over the earth." God not only gave Adam His own image and likeness; He gave him something Satan used to have—his old home and his old throne. Adam was now reigning on the earth from this same garden—the Garden of Eden. The final crushing blow to Satan's inflated ego was that Adam was in perfect fellowship with God.

In Genesis 3, we are told the voice of God would come and walk with Adam in the Garden in the cool of the day. A voice cannot walk unless that voice is a person, and the voice of God is none other than the Word of God, the eternal, sinless Son of God.

Adam was one with God.

Our Bible is the written Word; Jesus is the Living Word. God was fellowshipping with a lump of clay. Can you imagine the Word of God strolling into the Garden and saying to Adam, "Hey, you wanna hang?" Think of the stuff they must have talked about. It would have been amazing just to kind of hang from a tree and listen carefully to what they were saying.

Satan had that opportunity, and he listened intently to every word. He burned with jealousy, and he wanted to put a stop to God's plan. Somebody new had invaded Satan's space. This man, Adam, had been given dominion over the earth, and he wanted it all back. The more he listened, the more he seethed with jealous rage, until he could not bear it another second. He was determined to put an end to this nightmare that was a constant reminder of everything he had lost and what he could never have.

God didn't put Adam in the Garden to get in Satan's face. God made Adam in His image for a purpose, and Adam was given a commission:

> *Then God blessed them, and God said to them, "Be fruitful and multiply; fill the earth and subdue it; have dominion over the fish of the sea, over the birds of the air, and over every living thing that moves on the earth."*
>
> —GENESIS 1:28

God gave Adam His image because He wanted Adam to reproduce His image, filling the earth with sons of God and establishing His kingdom.

Satan lost it all, but do not think for one second that he lost his desire for God's crown or God's Kingdom. Satan was no dummy. He knew he had to move quickly to counter God before Adam could start reproducing other sons of God. The only way He could regain what he had lost was to get Adam to sin. Satan no doubt heard God tell Adam, "Of every tree of the garden you may freely eat; but of the tree of the knowledge of good and evil you shall not eat, for in the day that you eat of it you shall surely die" (Gen. 2:16-17). Satan heard that and knew what he had to do. If he could pull off getting Adam to eat of that tree, he would die spiritually. He would still have a living body and a living soul, but he would have a dead spirit. Adam would no longer be a trinity; he would no longer have the image of God, and therefore he would not be able to reproduce sons of

God. That meant there could be no Kingdom of God—only "sons of Adam"—sinful and fallen.

Of course you know the story. In Genesis 3, Satan went to Eve with the very same one-two punch he continues to use today. He attacked through lies, and he attracted through lust. I'll share more about the strategy of Satan later, but it is important to note that once he had set her up with lies and attracted her with lust, he came to her and baited her—the very same way he baits you and me. As we all know, Eve took the bait and Adam ate.

Genesis 5:3 is perhaps the saddest verse in the entire Bible: "Adam...begot a son in his own likeness, after his image." Adam's mission was aborted because of sin. For the next 4,000 years of human history spanning the entire Old Testament of your Bible, from the time that Adam sinned to the coming of Jesus Christ, no human being is ever again called a "Son of God." There were certainly believers in God, followers of God, and Abraham was called a "friend of God," but no one was ever again called a "Son of God." Because no one had the image of God, nobody could reproduce the image of God and establish His kingdom on the earth. But, God had a plan to redeem fallen man!

CHAPTER 3

ROUND THREE: BETHLEHEM'S MANGER

I will put enmity between you and the woman, and between your seed and her Seed; He shall bruise your head [the Resurrection], *and you shall bruise His heel* [the crucifixion].

—GENESIS 3:15

Second Corinthians 4:4 calls Satan, "the god of this age." He's only the little "g" god—not the big "G" God of the universe. Satan is powerful, but God is all powerful. Satan is mighty, but God is

Almighty. He is never wondering what He is going to do. He has always had a plan for His next move. Even while in the Garden of Eden, He was pronouncing judgment upon Satan, promising that one day a virgin-born Redeemer—the "Seed of the woman"—would come. God promised a Savior would emerge that would reverse the curse of sin for all men and redeem all of creation from Satan's dominion. Theologians call it the "incarnation"—God becoming a Man to be our sacrificial Lamb, but the prophet Isaiah would call Him "Immanuel" meaning "God with us" (Isa. 7:14).

Round three of this cosmic clash unfolds in the place of Jesus' birth, in the little town of Bethlehem. The kingdom had been abandoned—God's plan appeared to be aborted. First John 5:19 records, "The whole world lies under the sway [power] of the wicked one."

On this side of heaven, it looked like all was lost, but God knew what He was going to do before the foundations of the earth. Two thousand years ago in Bethlehem, a baby was being born. Everybody knows about the Christmas story and the nativity scene, but this pivotal event in the history of humanity is not so much about a baby lying in a manger as much as it is about the eternal, sinless Son of God coming in flesh and blood in fulfillment of God's promise recorded in Genesis 3:15.

In the beginning was the Word [Jesus], *and the Word was with God, and the Word was God... and the Word became flesh and dwelt among us.*
—JOHN 1:1,14

The Word of God that walked and talked with Adam in the Garden became flesh and blood. The last Adam is Jesus Christ (see 1 Cor. 15:45). God does not miss a thing, and He wants you to connect the dots and run the lines. He wants you to see the parallel. What the first Adam failed to do, the last Adam would finally accomplish. God's plan has always been intact, even when the first Adam's commission was canceled. God knew the last Adam was going to come to complete the commission the first Adam failed to fulfill. Satan had the upper hand on Adam's race. Where Adam's race was meant to rule, it was now Satan who reigned. The last Adam came to undo the curse of the first. And it is in Him that God's Kingdom will finally and forever be established.

The last Adam is more than "a" son of God; He is "THE" Son of God. He does more than simply reflect the image of God, He IS God; He is deity. Two thousand years ago, the eternal, sinless Son of God, the second Person of the Trinity, the Word of God, came in flesh and blood. That is why John 1:12 tells us, "But as many as received Him [Jesus], to them He gave the right to become children of God."

It is popular in our "enlightened" culture to say, "Well, we are all God's children, it does not matter who you are, it does not matter what you believe, it does not matter what God you worship, we are all God's children." NO, we are not! That's the lie of the devil himself. You are born the first time as a son of Adam. This is why Jesus said in John 3:3, "Unless one is born again, he cannot see the kingdom of God." Only then do you become a child and son of God. It is in Christ that we get back everything Adam lost because of sin. We regain the image of God, and we once again become a son of God.

We are not all God's children. If you have never placed your faith in Jesus Christ and given your life to Him, you have never been as Jesus said, "born again." He did not say you have to be a Baptist, Presbyterian, Methodist, or Pentecostal. He did not say you must be a Catholic; He did not say you must be whatever denomination you want to wear around your neck.

The question we must all answer is this: "Have you been born again?" You came into this world with a living body, a living soul, but a dead spirit. You do not bear God's image because you are not a trinity like God. You are born the first time after Adam's fallen image with Adam's fallen nature, but you are born the second time a recipient of God and Christ's divine nature.

The moment you place your faith in Jesus Christ, the Spirit of God gives life to your spirit. In an instant, you are born spiritually. You have a living body, a living soul, and a living spirit. You become a triune being to bear God's image and to be a part of God's Kingdom. God's plan for Christ to come was so somebody could finally reproduce God's image, and the only one who could fill the bill was God Himself.

In our intelligence gathering on the adversary, you cannot fully understand this battle of the ages without a deeper understanding of why it was so crucial to God's plan that He become a man. First, because dominion of the earth was lost by a man, it could only be redeemed by a man. The moment Adam sinned, dominion was transferred back to Satan, and no man could redeem the earth because no man was sinless. An angel could not do it—not a seraphim or cherubim or any other angelic creature.

Second, because it was the sin of a man that brought down the curse of sin, only the death of a sinless man could lift the curse of sin for all men. Romans 5:12 says, "Therefore, just as through one man sin entered the world, and death through sin, and thus death spread to all men, because all sinned." The problem was that no man could qualify to die for the sins of men, for all had sinned.

This is the fundamental difference that sets Christ apart from all other men. Jesus never sinned. Because He was born of a virgin, He had no earthly father—He was not a son of Adam. Therefore, He did not have Adam's fallen image or Adam's fallen nature.

Jesus was born of a virgin so that He would only have the image of His heavenly Father, which is divine, holy, and perfect. He was fully God, yet fully man. Because He never sinned, He was qualified to be the sacrifice for sin and lift the curse of sin from us all. Romans 6:23 tells us emphatically, "The wages of sin is death, but the gift of God is eternal life in Christ Jesus our Lord." Christ died for our sin and was buried, but three days later He rose from the dead and is alive forevermore.

Jesus scored the knockout punch in this battle of the ages. The devil is defeated because the grave could not hold Him. He has set us free from the slavery of sin and the tyranny of Satan. And most importantly, He will establish forever God's Kingdom.

Jesus said in John 8:36, "If the Son makes you free, you shall be free indeed." You come into this world in slavery and tyranny as a son of Adam, but you have been set free at the cross of Calvary. But Satan's strategy is to convince you that you are still living in bondage. Far too many Christians live their entire lives in captivity, never realizing they are in a prison of their own making. It is a lot easier to recognize the bars of our prison when we are captive to something like drugs or alcohol. But there are many, perhaps even you, who have succumbed to the lie that you are not smart enough, not pretty enough, and there is nothing you can do about it.

It only takes one heartbreakingly hurtful word or act to launch a vulnerable young girl into a life of promiscuity, anorexia, or bulimia. And men are just as susceptible. Too many give up and settle for where they are instead of breaking free to be all God created them to be. God did not create you to be a quitter, but a warrior and an overcomer. Male or female, there is a warrior on the inside of every one of us, and it is time to get on a war footing.

Throughout the New Testament, the Apostle Paul alludes to ministry being warfare. His writing is not allegory; he is being literal. He told Timothy he "must endure hardship as a good soldier of Jesus Christ" (2 Tim. 2:3), and to the Corinthians, the "weapons of our warfare are not carnal but mighty in God for pulling down strongholds" (2 Cor. 10:4), and so many more.

Many Christians understand there is a battle intellectually, but they do not really believe it practically. In fact, most people are already prisoners of war, and they do not even know it. My training on the police force as a member of the SWAT team prepared me for ministry by instilling in me a combat mentality. As we went through our training in the police academy, I once had a sergeant who would tell us over and over, "When you are in a gunfight, and you're in a fight for your life, you do not die until I give you permission to die!" He drilled that into us. He knew we were mostly a bunch of soft kids raised in the suburbs, and he was trying to prepare us with a true combat mentality. He would say, "If you get shot, you don't lie down; you continue to fight!" He would tell us that just because you take a hit doesn't mean you automatically fall down and die. That is just in the movies. In real life, you are not dead just because you are hit. You may take a hit, but you choose to live!

It is especially important for parents faced with the task of raising children to understand your children are facing a very real adversary. You must be vigilant and unyielding in your prayers. Bind every attack of the adversary from coming near them. Loose the angels of

God to encamp around them when they are at school, at the mall, or the movie theater. Lift up a prayer covering over them before they go off to school and when they lay their head down at night. Perhaps it's an older child who is far from God, and you're believing for their salvation. It might look like Satan is winning, but God has the final say. Never ever forget that Jesus is praying that your faith will not fail, and when God is for you, who can be against you?

Too many Christians have just the opposite mentality, and they go through life with a soft-target mentality. The first time they take a hit from one of Satan's "fiery darts," they fold. The next generation is growing up in an era of diplomacy and political correctness, only speaking words of peace and love. Certainly peace and love win in the end—but it is not the end! We are living in the age of warfare. Satan is a counterfeit king and temporarily the ruler of this world. He is still very much on the loose until Christ returns. We have a mortal enemy that wants to take us out every chance he gets.

Jesus said He came to set the prisoners free—that is you and me. Our position in Christ as children of God is one of victory. Jesus came out of the grave swinging a set of keys. Revelation 1:8, "I am the Alpha and the Omega, the Beginning and the End." And in Revelation 1:18, "I am He who lives, and was dead, and behold, I am alive forevermore...and I have the keys of Hades and of Death." Jesus has the keys to set you free from pornography, adultery, promiscuity, alcoholism, drug addiction, depression, pride, jealousy, and discouragement—whatever is holding you captive.

Satan is a thief, a liar, a murderer, and a robber, but he is also the ultimate loser in this war. Jesus Christ is the victor! As a born-again child of God, you do not have to live like a victim when you have been set free by the victor. The victor gets the spoils of warfare, and the souls of men and the souls of women are the spoils of this world.

God's plan has always been intact, and that is why you see the Bible come full circle. It ends right where it began. Most amazing of all is that what God would have done through the first Adam and Eve, He is now doing through the last Adam and His Eve. That is the reason the Church is called, the bride of Christ. As His bride, we are the "Eve" of the last Adam. A bride was necessary for Adam to fulfill the commission to be fruitful and multiply and fill the earth. That commission has never changed. Jesus gave the commission to His bride—His Eve, and He gave the commission to you and me right before He went back into heaven.

> *You shall receive power when the Holy Spirit has come upon you; and you shall be witnesses to Me in Jerusalem, and in all Judea and Samaria, and to the end of the earth.*
>
> —ACTS 1:8

As the bride of Christ, we are called to be "fruitful and multiply; fill the earth." Every time someone comes to faith in Jesus Christ and they are born again, they become a son or a daughter in the image of our heavenly

Father. That same battle that began long before Genesis 3 still rages today. It is the battle for a kingdom, a throne, and the world. All of the warfare, sin, suffering, and injustice of our world, back through the corridors of time, is but a reflection of this war for the world taking place at this very moment in the heavenlies.

I know when you look at our world, you wonder where God is in all this mess. I can promise you even though you may not be able to see it at this moment, God is diligently working all things for good according to Romans 8:28. Your heart may be troubled at times just like my heart is troubled as we look at the world and it seems to be "going to hell in a handbasket." In those times, take heart in Jesus' promise for us all:

> *Let not your heart be troubled; you believe in God, believe also in Me. In My Father's house are many mansions; if it were not so, I would have told you. I go to prepare a place for you. And if I go and prepare a place for you, I will come again.*
>
> —JOHN 14:1-3

There is coming a day when the last Adam is coming back again, and He is not coming empty-handed. He is coming with the title deed to this planet and what Revelation 5:5 calls a "seven-seal scroll." He bought it and redeemed it with His own blood on Calvary's cross. He is going to look at a squatter named Satan, and He is going to say, "Get off my land because I have the title deed." He is coming back this time not to wear a cross, but a crown. He came the first time to suffer, but He is coming back the second time to conquer. And the absolutely remarkable thing about how this war will end, the Bible says over and over again, is that we will rule and reign with Christ forever, and now you know why. The last Adam is going to rule and reign forever and ever, and we, His bride, are going to be at His side.

Every once in a while I like watching an old classic championship from some bygone era. ESPN will sometimes show an old Muhammad Ali fight or perhaps a Super Bowl matchup from 20 years ago. Recently something really got my attention as I sat down to unwind with a little ESPN. They were televising the 1988 NCAA basketball title game between the Kansas Jayhawks and the Oklahoma Sooners. I have blood and sweat equity in the Kansas football program, and I am still an unapologetic Kansas fan. (I'm sure some would say annoying, but I don't think so.) It was my freshman year in 1988 as I sat in my apartment with some of my friends watching Danny Manning and the Miracles take on the mighty Sooners. Now many years later, I sat in the living room of my home watching the rerun on ESPN. Suddenly, I was right back in my old apartment on campus again with the score tied 50-50 at halftime. What a game! I sat in my living room as the game wore on. I realized I was actually feeling the same case of nerves I experienced back in 1988. The adrenaline rush, the anxiety…Kansas might lose! I must admit I felt a little silly. I knew exactly how this game was going to end. The victory had already been won. Kansas defeated OU that night in 1988. All these years later I was watching the game again, but the end was no longer in doubt. I knew how it would end. No worries, we win.

The world is still at war with the adversary, but the end is not in doubt! The victory has already been won. Two thousand years ago, the Serpent Crusher scored the final blow! "Let not your heart be troubled," says Jesus (John 14:1). The rerun we are watching in time will one day soon catch up to eternity. His Kingdom will come and His will finally will be done on earth as it is in heaven. Amen.

The Apostle Paul said in First Corinthians 2:9, "Eye has not seen, nor ear heard, nor have entered into the heart of man the things which God has prepared for those who love Him." I cannot even imagine what that looks like, but I can promise it is going to be out of this world! One day soon, God's plan is going to be complete. He is going to bring to culmination His plan for the ages and bring eternal order to this cosmic chaos. All human suffering is because of the sin of men. Sin may have delayed the plan of God, but it will never destroy it. There is a day coming as wrecked and wicked as our world is, when paradise lost will become paradise regained.

PART II

THE ADVERSARY'S TACTICS

CHAPTER 4

KNOWLEDGE IS POWER

For we do not wrestle against flesh and blood, but against principalities, against powers, against the rulers of the darkness of this age, against spiritual hosts of wickedness in the heavenly places.

—EPHESIANS 6:12

We've looked at the theological, but now it's time to get highly practical. We have discovered why we find ourselves squarely in the middle of this battle of the ages. We now know the motivation behind Satan's relentless assault on God's Kingdom and God's people. It was his all-consuming pride that drove him to rebel against God, and he is the supreme sore loser. The battle still rages because he is still trying to steal the throne of God. He still has delusions of being worshiped as God and establishing his kingdom in place of God's Kingdom. Enough of Satan's lunacy!

We now must turn our attention to perhaps the most important part of our intelligence gathering on the adversary. In Paul's field manual for spiritual warfare, Ephesians chapter 6, he assures us that while every one of us is indeed at war with a very real enemy, we have weapons and we can win. Through our Christian Intelligence on the Adversary ("CIA"), we are going to learn how to live in victory over all the power of the enemy.

One of the fundamental principles of warfare is you never go to war without your body armor and your weaponry. As a rookie cop, I was mortified one night when I arrived to roll call. The entire way there I kept feeling like I had forgotten something. I couldn't figure out what, but something just didn't feel right. It was in the middle of roll call when I realized what I had done. My hands quickly snapped up to feel my chest. I had forgotten to put on my bulletproof vest! You'd better believe that night I did my best to "lay low."

The good news is God has equipped us with spiritual body armor. Paul is saying to us in Ephesians 6 that if you are going to stand against the wiles of the devil, it is essential you suit up with the whole armor of God. It is just as crucial to your victory to know your enemy because knowledge is power.

I'll never forget years ago catching a street dealer who was dealing drugs. I had watched him for several nights so I knew what he would do. I was watching him from a couple of blocks away. He never knew I was there. Every time a squad car turned the corner, I'd watch him turn to run inside the apartment building where he lived. There were two doors, and he always chose the one on the right. I knew it was time to make our move. By now, we knew what his move would be. I sat on the corner of the building in the shadows and radioed my partner to turn the corner in the squad car. Sure enough, he turned and ran for the door. About the time he reached for the door, I stepped out of the shadows and put a form tackle on him that would have made my old defensive line coach proud!

Knowing your enemy's moves is the secret to success on any level of warfare. It's why the United States has a Central Intelligence Agency (CIA) that is responsible for gathering intelligence information on our nation's adversaries. In 2015, the CIA uncovered a Russian spy operation going on right here in our own nation. While we were spying on them, they were busy spying on us. They had lived covertly among us posing as U.S. citizens for years, gathering intelligence information on the U.S. military and the U.S. government. And who can forget all the turmoil that ensued in 2016 when it was discovered Russian hackers had infiltrated some of the highest levels of government.

Opposing governments conduct espionage by sending spies secretly behind enemy lines to gain intelligence information for one reason: knowledge is power! It's no different for everyone fighting the good fight of faith. It is critical we are intimately acquainted with everything about our enemy.

The reason more Christians do not live victoriously is because they do not know Satan's strategy. Here's the reality—unless you gain knowledge about your enemy, you have no hope of succeeding against him. The prophet Hosea wrote about it thousands of years ago.

My people are destroyed for lack of knowledge.
—HOSEA 4:6

Those words are just as true in the spirit realm as they are in this earthly realm. The Bible tells us the devil has declared war on each of us. He has declared war on you. He is like the cartoon character, Wile E. Coyote who is always plotting and planning and strategizing to devour that innocent Road Runner. The Bible says that Satan really is a wolf—and one that is extremely wily. And just like Wile E. Coyote, he really does want to devour you. That is what Paul is teaching us and part of what we are doing in our intelligence gathering—learning about the wiles of the devil—the devices he employs in his assault against us and everything we hold dear.

Because we are at war, it is essential we continue our advanced intelligence gathering. As Paul says in Second Corinthians 2:11, "lest Satan should take advantage of us." If we do not learn about him and gather intelligence information about him, Satan WILL have the upper hand on us. Paul says we are not to be ignorant of his devices—his tools, his tricks, and his tactics—that he deploys against us.

The good news is—to use a little police jargon—we know his M.O., his modus operandi, his method of operation. Why? Because he has been using the only three bullets he has ever had since the dawn of humanity in the Garden of Eden—the lust of the flesh, the lust of the eyes, and the pride of life. And poor, naive Eve never saw it coming. As we study Genesis 3 in just a few turns of the page, we are going to see Satan's one-two combination. Like a trained boxer, he sets up his opponent with a jab and then goes for the knockout punch. First, he attacks through lies…then he attracts through lust. This is the one-two punch our adversary, the devil uses every time. He lures us in with lies and then baits the trap knowing the bait we're most apt to take.

It is probably safe to say you have taken the bait a time or two as well. I know I have. As a young teenager, I took the bait that began with a lie: "Phil, you aren't good enough and no girl would ever want you." Those thoughts and insecurities had me careening—if not for God's grace—toward a life wrecked by alcohol and womanizing. The lies I believed set me up to take the bait. What is the "bait" that Satan is using to lure you into his web of destruction? He may not be luring you down a path that will destroy your life, but one that will most certainly destroy your effectiveness for God's Kingdom. Is it one of bitterness? Or perhaps it's unforgiveness or anger that is searing your soul.

Just as crucial as knowing your enemy, it is essential you are gathering your information from a reliable source. Years ago as a member of the Kansas City SWAT, we would never serve a search warrant without first doing some intelligence gathering. Before we made a move, we would send a C.I., a confidential informant or undercover officer, to go to the location where the target was supposed to be. We would do that so they could report back to us as to what the house looked like, how it was laid out, whether there were any weapons or anything else we needed to be aware of.

On one particular occasion, we were getting ready to serve a drug warrant at an apartment. Our C.I. came back with intelligence information that our entry point was up the stairs and the first door on the left. We all heard and acknowledged his report and proceeded to charge up the stairs. On this occasion, I was the ram man, and BAM, I hit that first door on the left. However, as soon as that door came open, I realized something was terribly wrong. The only thing on the other side of that door was a 95-year-old man in nothing but his whitey tighties! The entire team was already in motion, proceeding with their finely tuned entry protocol. The first one inside the door pointed his gun at this poor man and yelled, "Get down, get down." Utterly petrified, the elderly man dove face down on the ground. As it turned out, we had received some bad intelligence. We found out later when our C.I. told us, "I meant the second door on the left, not the first one on the left. Sorry about that."

Now that was some pretty bad intelligence information. The good news is we always have good intel because our information comes from God Himself. Knowledge is power. God does not want us to be ignorant of Satan's devices. There is no more reliable source on the face of the earth than the Bible because it is inerrant, infallible, and it provides accurate intelligence on the enemy of our soul.

CHAPTER 5

A ROARING LION

Be sober, be vigilant; because your adversary the devil walks about like a roaring lion, seeking whom he may devour.

—1 PETER 5:8

Peter recognized that at the very core, Satan is a predator, and he is stalking you like you are what's for dinner. That means you had better be ready, and you had better be on guard. He wants to destroy you, and he wants to destroy everything you love.

If you are a born-again, blood-bought child of God, he cannot destroy your salvation for you have been redeemed by the sacrifice of God's Son, and you have been sealed by God's Spirit (see Eph. 4:30). What that means is he cannot take your soul to hell, but he wants to make your life a living hell. He cannot devour your soul, but he can devour everything else in your life—your peace, your joy, your health, your relationships—everything!

Think about that for a minute. If you know Satan is looking for someone to devour, you need to ask yourself if you're vulnerable to his attack. Are you being vigilant in guarding against his assault? Or have you been so wounded, so hurt that you are spending all your time and energy licking your wounds, telling yourself you aren't good enough, smart enough, pretty enough? If that's you, Satan is probably already dangling the bait you're most apt to take. What is it that will lure you into his snare? Someone who will really believe you are beautiful? That you are a man's man? That you're not stupid or ugly or fat or whatever wound has crippled you? Whatever it is, beware! You are an easy target for him to utterly and completely devour.

In our intelligence gathering, there is a lot we can learn from studying the habits of that kingliest of beasts. One of my favorite television programs when I was a little boy in the 1970s (yes, that's a long time ago) was Mutual of Omaha's Wild Kingdom. Those were the days before cable networks and Animal Planet. Entertainment options were limited, and I so looked forward to this show where the host would take us on wild safaris all over Africa. A really disappointing night for a ten-year-old kid would be 30 minutes of flamingos—especially since I'd been hoping all day for a show about the lions! Now that was going to be a good night of television! One learned right away why the lion was at the top of the food chain as the "king of beasts." He was the ultimate predator—cunning and patient as he stalked his prey.

A lion is extremely subtle in its intelligence gathering on its prey. The poor victim never knows the lion is lurking in the bush, never realizes the danger it is in until it's too late to escape. Make no mistake—Satan is coming after you; he is stalking you just like a lion stalks its prey. He is so subtle you will seldom even know he is there. That is the nature of Satan. You may not be studying his moves, but you better believe he is studying yours.

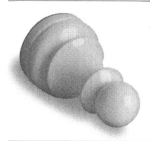

Just like that lion, Satan is patient. He does not care if he destroys you in a day or if it takes 20 years.

When a lion in the wild spots a herd of wildebeest or other prey, he doesn't immediately go charging down into the middle of them. A lion is in no hurry. In fact, he's likely to take all day surveying the landscape, watching and waiting, slowly and stealthily stalking his prey.

Just like that lion, Satan is patient. He does not care if he destroys you in a day or if it takes 20 years. He is as patient as he is relentless in his pursuit. You may not have him figured out, but he has you figured out. He is watching you and tracking your every move. He knows you, perhaps better than you know yourself. He knows every weakness and every wound. He knows where you are vulnerable and where you are strong. So he simply waits for the moment of weakness and vulnerability to attack. He slowly and subtly wears you down.

 He is looking to attack you with lies and then attract you with lust.

He is not omnipresent as is God, but he has a highly organized army of fallen angels assigned to specific regions of the world—cities, communities, and yes, even people—and that includes you. He is looking to attack you with lies and then attract you with lust. He is studying you to discover the bait you will fall for. Perhaps he sees how important it is to you to be the very best at what you do—the best mother, the best wife, the best dad, the best provider. He sees your drive to succeed, and he will lure you with more power and success until you lose your family in the process. You will be so distracted in pursuit of your goals, you'll never see him coming. And when you are still staggering from that first punch—when your husband walks out the door or you learn that your children are careening down the wrong path—Satan will come in with the knockout punch. For some, it may be promiscuity, drugs, or pornography. Many women find themselves in a prison of their own making with bars of debilitating depression, guilt, and any number of compulsive disorders that make them an easy target. Whatever it is—BEWARE!

The moment you make a mistake or drop your guard, Satan will leap into action—without remorse, without conscience, without repentance. He does not care about you—he wants to destroy you, and he wants to eat your life for lunch. He wants to have your leftovers for breakfast—that is the nature of a lion. He has no conscience, and he is not satisfied until your entire life has been consumed. So take heed to Peter's warning: "Be sober, be vigilant; because your adversary the devil walks about like a roaring lion, seeking whom he may devour" (1 Pet. 5:8).

Simply keeping a watchful eye is not enough. A lion preys on the weak, the sick, the vulnerable, and the isolated. A lion wants to isolate its prey from the rest of the herd. The Bible calls people sheep because they have no natural defenses against a predator. Sheep are vulnerable without a shepherd, but Christ is the Chief Shepherd. What He wants you to understand is as long as you are under the Chief Shepherd's authority, you have His protection upon your life so the lion cannot steal, kill, and destroy.

You are never more
vulnerable to the enemy
than when you're alone.

Sheep have no natural defenses—all they have going for them is to flock together. There is safety in numbers. A lion wants to isolate its prey. There might be hundreds of antelope in one place, but he will find the one that wanders off by itself. The animal that is isolated and alone has no one to come to his aid; he is utterly defenseless against the lion. It's the same for you. You are never more vulnerable to the enemy than when you're alone. When you quit going to church and you stop being around other Christians, you lose that umbrella of protection God has placed over your life. It is crucial that you are in a true biblical community of believers, part of the body of Christ! There is protection spiritually over your life simply by being a part of the body.

CHAPTER 6

THE MASTER ILLUSIONIST

Oh, that you would bear with me in a little folly—and indeed you do bear with me. For I am jealous for you with godly jealously. For I have betrothed you to one husband, that I may present you as a chaste virgin to Christ. But I fear, lest somehow, as the serpent deceived Eve by his craftiness, so your minds may be corrupted from the simplicity that is in Christ.

—2 CORINTHIANS 11:1-3

Satan is a counterfeiter of all that God does and all that God is. The Apostle Paul is telling the Corinthian church the very same thing he is telling you and me: Beware of the devil's deceptions! He counterfeits worship, he counterfeits religion, and he counterfeits all that is righteous and holy. He was a counterfeiter in the Garden of Eden in Genesis 3, and he continues his fakery today.

His deceptive reign will culminate very soon. The Bible records what will come upon the earth—a seven-year tribulation period when the Antichrist will emerge as a one-world ruler. Jesus said in Matthew 24 that he will go into the rebuilt Jewish temple, and he will proclaim himself to be the Messiah. He called it the "abomination of desolation." The entire world will worship him under the penalty of death (see Rev. 13), and he will deceive with "signs and lying wonders" (2 Thess. 2:9). For a short season, he will have what he has been warring for since launching his insurrection with the words, "I will ascend into heaven...." He will sit on the throne of God, be worshiped as God, and reign over an earthly kingdom like God. He will deceive the masses by counterfeiting even the miracles of God.

If you want to understand how Satan assaults and deceives you and me, it is crucial you study Genesis 3. It is a textbook case in our intelligence gathering on the adversary. Genesis 3 is not a myth. The Garden of Eden was a real place, and Adam and Eve were real people. We are living in a culture where the average American does not believe Genesis 3 really happened. They do not believe in a literal Adam or a literal Eve. Even if you don't want to think biblically about it, think logically. The very fact that there are over seven billion human beings on our planet demands there had to be a first

man and a first woman. Scripture tells us their names—
Adam and Eve. Many today no longer believe in a literal
Satan. If you are like so many others who simply believe
Satan is no more than the figment of some religious
people's imagination or simply a symbol of evil, you are
the worst kind of prisoner—you are a prisoner *unaware!*

Satan's greatest tactic in 21st-century America is to
convince multitudes of men and women he is not real. If
you do not believe in Satan because you are so enlightened, you are going to have to rip out almost every book
in your Bible. You will have to rip out all of Genesis
because Satan's in there; you will have to rip out most
of the prophets in the Old Testament because they all
wrote about Satan; you will have to rip out most of your
New Testament—Peter, James, John—because they all
wrote about Satan; and you will have to rip out the Gos-
pels—Matthew, Mark, Luke and John—because Jesus
talked more about Satan than almost any other subject.

If you are going to say Satan is not real, you better be
careful because you are also saying that Jesus was either
a liar or a lunatic. If you are going to say Satan is not
real, you have no Bible left. So you can see why he wants
to convince you he is not real.

> *Now the serpent was more cunning than any beast
> of the field which the Lord God had made. And
> he said to the woman, "Has God indeed said,
> 'You shall not eat of every tree of the garden'?"
> And the woman said to the serpent, "We may eat
> the fruit of the trees of the garden; but of the fruit*

of the tree which is in the midst of the garden, God has said, 'You shall not eat it, nor shall you touch it, lest you die.'" Then the serpent said to the woman, "You will not surely die. For God knows that in the day you eat of it your eyes will be opened, and you will be like God, knowing good and evil." So when the woman saw that the tree was good for food, that it was pleasant to the eyes, and a tree desirable to make one wise, she took of its fruit and ate. She also gave to her husband with her, and he ate.

—GENESIS 3:1-6

Remember Satan's three-step attack. His strategy against Eve in Genesis 3 is the same strategy he uses today against you and me.

1. He disguises his appearance.

2. He deceives with lies.

3. He distorts man's mind.

Satan is a master illusionist; he has multiple disguises. Eve was immediately deceived because he always comes in disguise. Forget all the mental images you have of Satan being a scary-looking person—that is not who Satan really is when he comes to attack. He did not come to her as a talking snake wrapped around a tree. That makes for really good coloring books for six-year-olds in Sunday school, but she did not see a talking snake.

If you go into your garden tomorrow morning and you encounter a talking snake in your garden, you are going to be scared. I am not too brave to admit that I am going to be scared. In fact, I am going back to the house. And you can forget me picking any tomatoes tomorrow either if there is still a talking snake in the garden! Here's the point: Eve did not see a talking snake. The record of Eve in Genesis is not one of fear and apprehension. She appeared to be not in the least bit fearful of who she was talking to and whatever she was seeing.

Genesis 3:1 tells us, "Now the serpent was more cunning than any beast of the field..." Satan is associated with the beast of the field, not with creeping things. If he was a snake and that was what she was seeing, he would be associated with Genesis 1:24—"creeping" things. The serpent in Genesis 3 is the same serpent of Revelation 12:9 who will one day soon supernaturally empower the beast of Revelation 13. That beast is none other than the Antichrist. He will emerge onto the world scene as a world ruler during the seven years of tribulation. He is said to be a beast, not in his appearance but in his identity.

One of Satan's primary strategies is to come disguised as something that will be acceptable to his prey. In the Garden of Eden, he came to Eve in a form that was familiar and acceptable to her. Today, he comes as someone who cares about you and what you are going through, only to tear you down at the first opportunity. He is the gold digger who only wants your money and the wolf in sheep's clothing who wants to sell you a bill of goods. He's the shoulder to lean on when your heart is broken, only to take advantage of you. He's the other woman or man who is tearing your marriage apart. He's the partner who is robbing your business blind and the conniving coworker who wants your job.

The first step in Satan's attack is to disguise his appearance.

He will deceive the world in exactly the same way he deceived Eve—by cunningness and craftiness. Daniel 8:25 speaks about the Antichrist, the beast of Revelation 13: "Through his cunning he shall cause deceit to prosper under his rule." He will deceive the world and masses of humanity. Second Thessalonians 2:9 tells us it will be "with all power, signs, and lying wonders." We are living in a day and age when so many people are mesmerized by the miraculous. They are chasing signs and wonders at every opportunity. I thoroughly believe God is still a God of wonders. He is still a God of the miraculous. But if you are trying to discern the work of God based on signs and wonders, I have to warn you: Satan can do those too!

I thoroughly believe our God has never stopped being a God of miracles. He is the God that parted the Red Sea, He brought manna down from heaven, and

He brought water from a rock. Yes, He is the God of the supernatural, but if you are looking to authenticate the work of God through signs and wonders and supernatural miracles, you are setting yourself up to be deceived. During the tribulation, Satan will deceive millions and millions in this way (see 2 Thess. 2:9). Satan knows human beings are suckers for what they see. That is how he deceived Eve. She went on what she saw rather than what God had said.

Just because you see something that appears to be supernatural, it does not mean it is automatically of God. Satan can manifest signs and wonders too. That is why First John 4:1 tells us to "test the spirits, whether they are of God," because there is more than the Holy Spirit at work in this world. There are also demonic, deceiving spirits at work. If you encounter anything that contradicts the Word of God, it is not the work of the Spirit of God. You know it is a counterfeit and not of God.

The problem is that Satan knows we are easily deceived by appearances. He knows our nature as human beings is to trust in what we can see. We determine whether something is real and true based on sight. Most people never get beyond "what meets the eye." They see the obvious but miss the "not so obvious." First Samuel 16:7 says, "Man looks at the outward appearance, but the Lord looks at the heart." Satan disguises his appearance because he knows that is as far as most human beings will ever look.

We must see behind the mask to see who's in disguise and discern whether or not it is Satan, Jesus said in John 7:24, "Do not judge according to appearance, but judge with righteous judgment." Eve was immediately deceived because she judged according to appearance. She judged according to what she could see instead of what God said. The moment the first words came out of his mouth, she should have immediately known this was an imposter. She shouldn't have cared who he was or what he was, and the conversation should have been over. But she did not judge with righteous judgment—she judged according to appearance.

In John 7:24, Jesus was talking about the importance of having discernment between truth and error, right and wrong, between false doctrine and pure doctrine, between the work of God and the work of Satan. Just because something sounds good does not mean it is truly from God. You cannot truly discern what is of God apart from the Word of God.

In your Christian intelligence gathering, you must learn to base everything you think, see, hear, and feel on what the Bible says. It is the reason God has given us the Bible. Jesus said in John 17:17 as He prayed to the Father on our behalf, "Sanctify them by Your truth. Your word is truth." The Bible is our God-given guide to help us discern between right and wrong and good and evil. It is our final authority. It gets the last say. You hold it up as the absolute standard for truth regardless of what you see. If you do not learn to base what you think and what you believe on what God has said, you will be deceived every time. If you want to live the abundant life of God, it is crucial you learn to weigh everything through the lens of Scripture and not your own understanding.

So how exactly did Satan deceive Eve? First and foremost she did not pay attention to the Word of God. As a result, she was fooled into thinking this was the work of God. The moment Satan questioned the Word of God saying, "Has God indeed said?" she should have immediately known it wasn't the work of God.

What disguise and what distortion of his appearance did he use? What exactly did Eve see? I can assure you she did not see a snake. Genesis 3:1 says, "Now the serpent was more cunning than any beast of the field." When you read and study the Word of God, you have to measure every single word. It is not just the thoughts or general ideas of God, it is called the Word of God. It is important to notice this passage refers to "the" serpent because it is talking about a person. It does not say, "a" serpent because it is not referring to just any old serpent. It says "the" serpent because it is talking about some*body*, not some*thing*.

"Serpent" is simply an identity—not what he looked like. Just to make sure we do not miss the connection, God gives us Revelation 12:9 to clarify it for us: "So the great dragon was cast out, that serpent of old, called the Devil and Satan, who deceives the whole world; he was cast to the earth, and his angels were cast out with him."

In Second Corinthians 11:3, Paul says "the serpent" deceived Eve. The context in which he is writing has to do with how Satan deceived Eve and how he is worried that you and I will be deceived in exactly the same way. In verse 14, he says Satan "transforms himself into an angel of light."

CHAPTER 7

AN ANGEL OF LIGHT

In other parts of the world, Satan's primary tactic is persecution. He wants to devour through fear, intimidation, or persecution in places like North Korea, the Islamic world, and Red China where Christians are persecuted. In the United States of America, his principal tactic against our society is not that of persecution. To the contrary— he comes as an angel of light rather than a roaring lion, and his primary tactic is deception. In Second Corinthians 11:13-14 Paul writes, "For such are false apostles, deceitful workers, transforming themselves into apostles of Christ. And no wonder! For Satan himself transforms himself into an angel of light."

Many Hebrew scholars tell us the Hebrew word "nachash," from which the word "serpent" is translated, originally meant "shining one." Originally, Lucifer was the light bearer—the shining one. In all probability, Eve thought she was looking at the preincarnate Christ Himself, the Messiah. But it was a counterfeit Christ, it was an antichrist.

He comes as an angel of light rather than a roaring lion, and his primary tactic is deception.

Satan is the ruler over the powers of darkness (see Eph 6:12). But in his pre-fallen condition, he is called, "Lucifer, son of the morning" or "light bearer" (see Isa. 14). He was created by God to bear the light of God, but when he sinned he lost the title "light bearer." Now he rules not over light but over darkness as the ruler of darkness. His domain is in the things we do not want anyone to know about—those things that are done in secret. He is stalking you on every aspect of media, lurking in the recesses of the internet. It is no coincidence that one of the most insidious parts of the internet is called the "dark" web—a secretive part of the regular web that has become a haven for drug markets, pedophiles, and sex traffickers.

This one-time archangel has now become a dark angel. Paul says to watch out because he still transforms himself into an angel of light. He wears many masks, and he is the master of deception. That means all that glitters is not gold, and just because something sounds good does not mean it is of God.

So tell us, Paul, what is it exactly that Eve saw in Genesis 3 at the tree? Paul tells us Eve saw a glorious, beautiful godlike being. Satan's greatest deception is he disguises himself as God, and on this day in Genesis 3, Eve saw an angel of light—a beautiful godlike being.

Many a young girl has been deceived by the good looks and charming ways of a young man, only to be left with a baby to raise alone. One of the primary tactics of sex traffickers is to convince a young college student they are from a modeling agency or movie-making enterprise, luring them into a place from which they can never escape. How many women have been trapped in marriages where they were beaten black and blue, unable to leave because they are convinced, "He didn't really mean to do it. He's really a good person."

He's the business partner that is a so-called Christian but operates with no integrity or moral values in his business dealings. She's the teacher in your children's school teaching there is no God, no right or wrong, and everybody is a winner. She's the yoga instructor opening the door to New Age practices and the occult. He's the football coach who everyone thinks is a hero who is molesting innocent boys in the shower and leading them down a path of destructive behavior. Can you hear the serpent's *hisssssss?*

Satan deceived Eve in exactly the same way he is going to deceive masses of humanity during the tribulation. Revelation 13 tells us he will introduce to the world an antichrist, a counterfeit Christ, who will appear so much like Christ Himself that Jesus said in Matthew 24:24, "If possible, even the elect" will be deceived. Jesus was saying he will look and act like Christ—even doing supernatural miracles—in an attempt to deceive even the elect.

In Genesis 3:8, it is implied that Adam and Eve would walk with the voice of the Lord in the Garden in the cool of the day. No wonder she was not alarmed. No wonder she had no hint of fear or insecurity. She had walked with the voice of God, the Son of God, over and over again. She was not alarmed because Satan appeared to her to be like God Himself. She based her judgment solely on what she could see rather than what he said. What she could see was not Christ; it was a counterfeit...an antichrist. The moment he opened his mouth and said, "Has God indeed said, 'You shall not eat of every tree?'" Eve immediately should have said, "I do not know who you are, I do not know what you are, you look like Him but you are not Him—this conversation is over." But she did not. She was tricked by what she saw, she did not listen to what he said, and the world is still reeling from that diabolical deception. We can only imagine what a different world this would be if only she had recognized that angel of light for what he truly was—the devil himself. We have been falling for his lies ever since.

In Second Corinthians 11, Paul is teaching that the same way he attacked Eve is the same way he attacks you and me—by disguising his appearance. He is a master illusionist. You must learn to measure everything you see, everything you hear, everything you feel, and everything you experience not on what you see but on what God has said. Why? Because Satan is a lot like the professional illusionists we see today. Their entire livelihood is based on the fact that your eyes can deceive you.

Jesus warned in Matthew 24:4-5, "Take heed that no one deceives you. For many will come in My name, saying, 'I am the Christ,' and will deceive many." These days, you can't take anything at face value. From impostors to scammers to con artists, they all weave their webs of deception. You cannot believe everything you see or hear. Seeing is not believing. Things are not always as they appear. The only thing that is true is the Word of God. John 17:17 declares, "Your word is truth." You can solidly stand on it with absolute confidence, knowing that God will fulfill every word He has spoken.

Whether we want to admit it or not, it is easy to be deceived. I remember going to carnivals or the circus where there would always be people who would lead you to believe they had gifts or special powers they used with their fortune-telling, palm reading, and tarot card reading. Their powers were either inspired through demonic forces or they were doing nothing more than playing tricks on you.

I've even seen people on talk shows that appear to be communicating messages from the dead. They are using the same tricks of the trade that can be purchased from various websites and catalogs. Matthew 24:24 says that false christs and false prophets will come with grand illusions. Again, it's easy to deceive. Don't put your trust in false prophets who carry a Bible or sling scripture to appease the masses. Make sure your foundation is securely anchored in the infallible Word of God. Arm yourself so you are not deceived by having a solid knowledge of the scriptures. In Second Corinthians 5:7 it says, "We walk by faith, not by sight." Your eyes can deceive you so test the spirits and ensure they are of God (see 1 John 4:1).

I enjoy watching a professional illusionist from time to time. When you watch an illusionist, you will see things you did not really see, such as a man with a pitcher of water that never ran dry. You might have thought you saw a man read the minds of others or levitate a table, but it did not really happen. That is what a master illusionist does. But they are called "illusionists" for a reason. It was all an illusion. Your eyes tricked your brain into seeing things that looked real but weren't real.

There is an illusionist who is far more masterful than what we might see at a magic show. He distorts his appearance because he knows that most human beings will base what they believe on what they see instead of what God has said.

If you do not want to be deceived in this deceptive age, you must come to the place where you trust what God has said regardless of what you see. Eve based what she "thought" was real only on what she could see. She was immediately deceived because she did not pay attention to what God had said. The moment anybody opens their mouth and questions the Word of God, somehow denies the Word of God, or casts doubt on the Word of God, there should be alarms going off and red lights flashing in your head. You should immediately recognize it is not the Spirit of God—it is a deceiving spirit.

In fact, you probably encounter that deceiving spirit far more than you realize. It is no surprise that many ancient cultures, like the Mayans, worshiped a winged serpent. A winged serpent looks a lot like a dragon, which not so coincidently is associated with China. It's one of Satan's disguises.

In Genesis 3:1, he is identified with the beast of the field. "Beast" in the Bible is always associated with cattle. It should come as no surprise that cattle were worshiped by ancient people. The Israelites coming out of Egypt learned to worship a golden calf while they were still enslaved. There are still many people in the world, like the Hindus, who continue to worship cattle.

Today in America, Satan does not deceive us with cattle, bulls, or oxen. He does not disguise himself as a winged serpent or as a dragon. We are much too educated, and we are certainly not superstitious. We are far too sophisticated after all to be deceived by a snake. He uses far more subtle disguises to mask his true identity.

Oftentimes it could be the kindest, most compassionate person you have ever seen in your life. He does not look anything like Satan; she does not act anything like the devil. She cares about people, she loves people, but the moment she casts doubt on the Word of God, she is no longer being used by the Spirit of God. Do not base your sense of reality on what you can see but only on what God has said.

Satan is extremely religious, and it's one of his most effective disguises. Over and over again in the Bible he is found quoting Scripture, but when he does, he is quoting it out of context. He is twisting it and contorting it just as he does today with those who will contort God's Word.

It could be the Jehovah's Witnesses or the Mormons standing on your doorstep. They are certainly seen cloaked in religion and quoting Bible verses, but they deny the deity of Jesus Christ. First John 2:22 says, "Who is a liar but he who denies that Jesus is the Christ? He is antichrist who denies the Father and the Son." It is not the Spirit of Christ; it is the Spirit of antichrist.

My purpose is not to attach the serpent to any person but to a doctrine. Mormons, Jehovah's Witnesses, and members of the New Age movement are not our enemies—Satan is. They are good people who have been deceived. Don't treat anyone like an enemy when the real enemy is always the one we can't see, pulling the strings behind the scenes.

He can be found working behind the scenes in the so-called "church" with the sweet-sounding pastor who long ago denied the authority of Scripture. Churches all across America deny the authority of the Bible, no longer truly believing it is the Word of God. Many churches in this land do not truly stand on the foundation of the Bible; they no longer believe it is infallible, that it is perfect. They do not believe it is inerrant or without error. They do not really believe it is God-breathed and that it is, in fact, written by God above. They think it is somehow just written by men—a book of good ideas and good suggestions, but it is not really the final authority.

The moment anyone begins to doubt the Word of God or cast doubt on the Word of God or deny the authority of the Word of God, it does not matter how sweet sounding they are or how religious they look. They are not being used by the Spirit of God, and they are under the delusion of the deceiving spirit.

How does Satan disguise himself in 21st-century America? It is the celebrity with his or her New Age theology who says you have no need of a Savior; there is no sin, just look at the divinity within. It is Oprah Winfrey and all of her New Age friends. Is she a great philanthropist? Yes. Does she care about humanity? Yes, but that is not the point. The New Age theology will send millions and millions to hell. It is her friend, Eckhart Tolle, and his book *The New Earth* that says you have no need of a Savior, you do not need salvation, just look at the divinity within.

Here's the remarkable thing about New Age theology—there is nothing new about it. It goes back to the Garden of Eden. "Hey Eve, if you eat of this tree, you can be like me, you can be like God." There is nothing new about New Age theology. It is Tom Cruise and Kirstie Alley with their Church of Scientology—"We are the only salvation we ever need, just look within, there is no sin." *Hssssssssssss!*

It is the movement to unite the world religions. Oh, it sounds good, but everything that sounds good is not always of God. It seeks to bring the world religions together. "Forget about our differences; let us just come together in the name of acceptance and love and tolerance. After all, all religions lead to heaven. Jesus, Buddha, Allah, it does not matter. They all lead to God. It does not matter who you worship or what you believe, everyone is eventually going to get to heaven." *Hsssssssssss...*

The problem is that Jesus said in John 14:6, "I am the way, the truth, and the life. No one comes to the Father except through Me." He made an absolute, exclusive claim in Acts 4:12, "There is no other name under heaven given among men by which we must be saved." The reason Jesus is the only way is because He is the only one in history who ever died for your sin. Mohammed did not die for your sin, Allah did not die for your sin, and Buddha certainly did not die for your sin. Jesus could say He is the only way because He is the only one who ever died for your sin on the cross of Calvary. The moment anybody says that Jesus is "*A*" way but not the "*only*" way, you know immediately it is not the work of God because they are denying the Word of God. Does it sound good? Yes. Who wouldn't like to get along? It sounds good, but all that sounds good is not always of God.

Satan is disguising his appearance over and over again. He comes through the enlightenment. Aren't you glad that now we are an enlightened people, no longer superstitious like those that came before us? Aren't you glad we are so much smarter now than prior generations? It is intellectualism. It is naturalism. It is secular humanism and the evolutionary lie that says there is no Christ but the cosmos. The cosmos is all that is, or was, or will ever be. There is only the universe; there is no God, there is no creator, and there is only the cosmos. The universe is all that was or will ever be. *Hssssssssssss!* It is all the deceptive lies of Satan himself.

We are living in a world that is shrouded in deception and darkness. If you want to see in the darkness, you need the light. When I was a member of Kansas City SWAT, we had something called night vision—goggles that helped to see in the night. As believers, we have the same thing—the Word of God. Psalm 119:105 tells us, "Your word is a lamp to my feet and a light to my path." You can only see in the darkness of the night by holding up the light. The light is God's Word—your night vision. Only as you put on the night vision, measuring everything you see through the lens of Scripture, can you avoid being deceived.

Not only do we have night vision, but I like to say we have light sabers. Why? As children of the light, we are at war with the kingdom of darkness. We can only prevail in this warfare with the kingdom of darkness as we go forth in the power of the light. The "sword of the Spirit" is our night vision and our light saber.

CHAPTER 8

HELL'S HAYMAKER: SATAN'S ONE-TWO PUNCH

Satan has always had a one-two punch. It is the same jab and cross combination he used on Eve that he uses on you and me. From Genesis 3 to the 21st century, it has always been his signature move.

He will set you up with a volley of lies just like a boxer. When I went on the PD, I had never actually been in a real fight. You might say I had lived a rather sheltered life, and growing up I had always gotten along with just about everybody. The few guys that didn't like me didn't really want to meet "out back" either since I was usually a full head taller than everybody else, with a reputation on the football field. I probably wasn't as tough as they thought, but it didn't matter since nobody really challenged me for the "title." When I entered the police academy, they immediately began teaching us some basic hand to hand and martial arts skills like wrist locks and reverse punches.

It was when I entered the SWAT team that I learned to box. They knew a lot of us had never been punched in the face; we had never been in a real fight. If you're going to be a member of the SWAT team, you need to learn how to take a punch. When you're a cop, your life may depend on it! It's equally true spiritually in the "ring" of life. You don't fold just because your opponent draws blood. SWAT training included learning how to take a punch—and deliver one too. One day we put on our gloves and headgear and squared off with our partner. The bell rang and we went at it. Wow, it was fun! At 6'6", my partner knew to try to come in low to get inside my long reach. I really didn't have any idea what I was doing. Had I been thoroughly trained, I would have come at him with an uppercut. Instead, I just came down on top of his head with a big tomahawk chop. It was hardly a form of boxing, but it worked. His headgear didn't protect the top of his head and it knocked him out cold. He just dropped straight down and sat on the mat with his chin on his chest until he woke up a few seconds later. That was the last time they ever let us box.

What I learned before they "suspended" my boxing career were the basic boxing combinations. There are several, but the most basic punches are the #1 and the #2. The #1 is the jab and the #2 is the cross. It's the one-two combination where you jab your opponent with your weak side and then cross punch him with your power side. It's the cross punch that is the knockout, not the jab. The jab just sets up the cross punch.

This is how Satan works to take us out. A trained boxer never begins with the big cross punch throwing the big "haymaker." That only happens in the movies. (Sorry to disappoint all the Rocky fans.) If he tries throwing a big roundhouse punch right out of the chute, he knows he is going to miss because his opponent will see it coming. What does he do? He first sets up his opponent with a volley of jabs. That is exactly what Satan does. He sets you up with a volley of lies in order to wear you down. Finally, when you are hanging on the ropes of life from his barrage of lies, he brings the big haymaker—the knockout punch. He dangles the bait you're most apt to take.

THE FATHER OF LIES

Now the serpent was more cunning than any beast of the field which the Lord God had made. And he said to the woman, "Has God indeed said, 'You shall not eat of every tree of the garden'?"
—GENESIS 3:1

First Satan attacked Eve by disguising his appearance, but his second step was to deceive Eve with lies. Notice he's far too wise to begin with an obvious lie. He begins by just asking Eve a question: "Did God really say...?" If someone in your life were to tell you, "There is no God," there is a good chance (since you're reading this book) you would never believe that lie. That's way too obvious. You would never really doubt the existence of God. The most dangerous lies are the "subtle" ones. Perhaps, "Maybe God doesn't really care." In all probability, you've already pondered that possibility at some point in your life. "There is no God" and "God doesn't really care" are both equally untrue. However, one is far more believable than the other based on our circumstances. Satan knows this all too well. This is always how Satan goes on the attack. He simply takes a subtle jab at the truth of who God is or what God says. Think about it. Satan's very first recorded words in Scripture are a question. He does not initially attack the Word of God; he doesn't even deny the Word of God. That would have been much too obvious to Eve.

Instead, Satan simply takes a subtle jab at God's Word. "Eve, did God really say you shall not eat of every tree?" He just planted a seed of doubt in Eve's mind about what God had actually said. He did not deny what God said; he did not attack what God said. He simply posed the question, "Has God indeed said...?" He wanted her to doubt the reliability, the accuracy, the authority, and the acceptability of what God said.

Is it any wonder that the Bible itself and Bible-believing Christians are under such attack? There is more hostility today toward the Bible than there has ever been in history. You see, this battle of the ages has always been about the truth and infallibility of God's Word.

The second step in Satan's attack is to deceive with lies.

The only way Satan can win this war is to convince you to embrace his lies instead of the truth of what God has said. Jesus tells us in John 8:44 that Satan "is a liar and the father of it." He has been lying since the beginning in Genesis 3, and he continues to lie today. He attacks through lies because Jesus said "there is no truth in him" (John 8:44). It is the only way he can defeat you daily, and it is the only way he can defeat you practically. The lies of the enemy then become your false reality. And like Eve, that false reality will become your captivity. If Satan can get you to *doubt* the Word of God, he can eventually get you to *deny* the Word of God. Once he has succeeded in getting you to deny God's Word, he has you right where he wants you. It is the strategy he used to attack Eve, and it is the strategy he uses to attack you and me.

The biggest problems facing our nation are moral and spiritual. We are a nation in spiritual chaos, spiritual crisis, spiritual confusion, and spiritual anarchy. As a society, we have abandoned the Word of God as our ultimate authority. We are not, as some say, becoming a godless nation, but rather we are tragically becoming a nation of many gods. We are becoming a nation that is theologically pluralistic. Jesus is "a" way, but He is not THE ONLY way. There is Buddha, Allah, Mohammed, Confucius—or just go worship a tree. It does not matter because "all paths lead to God." One is as good as another. That is spiritual anarchy. And therefore, we are a nation in spiritual confusion. It all begins when you lose the anchor and the authority of what God has said.

Not only are we living in a time of spiritual anarchy, we are living in a time of moral anarchy. From rising divorce rates, to redefining marriage, to STDs, homosexuality, sexual immorality—to promiscuity, pornography, unwanted pregnancies, racism, inequality, and rising violence among our teens—any semblance of moral absolutes in our society have gone by the wayside. It's as though our society has decided there is no such thing as sin. No moral absolutes of right and wrong. It is all the reflection of a nation that has lost its moral anchor and no longer holds true to the absolute words of what God has said. It did not just happen yesterday. Like that roaring lion, Satan has been stalking our nation for decades, tempting its people with one tantalizing bait after another, as he leads America down a path of destruction and desolation.

As I wrote earlier, Satan disguises his appearance, and he shows up in the most unlikely of places—even in the Bible colleges and the seminaries of this nation with professors with PhD behind their name who do not believe in the absolute truth of what God has said. Multiple thousands of young preachers and would-be pastors went to these Bible colleges and seminaries and heard their professor say things like, "We are not really sure you can take everything the Bible says literally." I am sure you have heard someone say, "Well, you can't take that literally" when the Bible says something they don't like or don't agree with. After disguising his appearance, Satan's next step is always to deceive with lies. His favorite lie is, "Well you can't really take the Bible seriously. You can't take it literally."

I wonder how much you like it when your kids do that to you. "Mom, I didn't know when you said to take out the trash you really meant that literally." Or, "Dad, I didn't know when you said to be home by midnight you wanted me to take you seriously." Come on...what kind of a parent would let their kids get away with that? When you tell your kids to do something, you want them to take you seriously. I learned a lot from my father growing up. I learned early on that the "gluteus maximus" is directly connected to the "cerebral cortex"! When I failed to take my dad seriously and obey what he said, he would stimulate my gluteus maximus. I would get a whole new revelation in my cerebral cortex! I am thankful I learned to take my father at his word. It helped me learn to take my heavenly Father at His word as well.

When God said what He said, He meant what He said. Yes, there is symbolism in Scripture, but when God is speaking symbolically, He will always make it obvious.

By comparing Scripture with Scripture, we can discern the meaning behind the symbolism. When you do, you quickly learn the Bible is a self-defining and self-interpreting book. Jesus' teaching was full of symbolism. He presented Himself as a Shepherd, Sower, Bridegroom, Door, Cornerstone, Vine, Light, Bread, and Water.

The Bible has figurative language, but it is far more literal than most people think. Beginning in the early 20th century, as many American seminaries were drifting from the belief in biblical inerrancy, future pastors and church leaders were being taught they could not trust their Bible because it wasn't really reliable. This led to the modern era of "cut and paste" theology being practiced by most of America's clergy and churches. It is an insidious lie of the adversary that we have the authority to pick and choose what parts of the Bible are the Word of God and which parts aren't, based on our own arbitrary ideas and opinions. Yet whatever is found in the pulpits eventually finds its way into the pews. This "cut and paste" theology is no different than what was going on in Genesis 3. Satan disguises his appearance with religious-looking clergy saying religious-sounding things, while they subtly (and sometimes not so subtly) attack the reliability of what God has said. It's in Second Timothy 3:5: "having a form of godliness but denying its power." No wonder the Church in America is powerless to impact society. Satan has effectively disarmed the Church. When you deny the Word of God, you lose the power of God! Can you hear the serpent's *Hsssssssss?*!

And we wonder why the youngest generation is leaving the Church in droves as our nation becomes more and more secular. If you want your kids to embrace the faith and stay active in church long after they grow up, then give them something to believe in! Yet entire denominations are slowly dying out, and they can't figure out why all their young people are leaving. Why would they stay when they've been taught NOT to believe? Instead, let's give them something to believe!

Here is the simple truth. Isaiah 40:8 shouts it: "The grass withers, the flower fades, but the word of our God stands forever." Everything in this world is fleeting; nothing's going to last forever, but the Word of God. It will last for eternity when the world has evaporated into history. The Word of God is a solid rock of ultimate and eternal truth that will still be standing when everything else has faded away. Jesus made the promise in Matthew 5:18, "For assuredly, I say to you, till heaven and earth pass away, one jot or one tittle will by no means pass from the law till all is fulfilled." For all the "red letter" Christians that claim only the words in "red" spoken directly by Jesus Himself are authoritative, it might be worth remembering what Jesus was talking about when He said these words—he was referring to the Old Testament. Yes, that includes those parts of Scripture that even some professing Christians appear to hate and attack as unreliable and outdated or antiquated. Jesus was promising divine preservation of the Scriptures, including the Old Testament, that is so often attacked today by even those within the Church. He was promising it would be preserved to even the smallest detail. Nothing will be lost from God's Word. Be careful before you attack any part of the Bible. Jesus believed it ALL!

Some say, "But you have to choose between being a person of faith or a person of reason." Don't you hear that a lot these days? It's the serpent's Hsssssssss. "In this age of scientific enlightenment, we now know..." Hssssssssss... "Well, it's either science or faith." Hssssssssss... There are many who would have you think only a backwoods "hillbilly" still believes the Bible. I can say with all confidence there is no contradiction or conflict whatsoever between the Bible and science or being a person of faith and a person of reason. God created the universe and the scientific laws that govern the universe. Isaiah 1:18 says, "Come now, and let us reason together..." I am going to be honest with you. I think I am a man of at least average intelligence. I have a college education from one of the finest public institutions in all the land (with a pretty fine basketball tradition too). With my dying breath, I am going to defend the authority and the inerrancy and the infallibility of the Bible.

The battle of the ages has always been a battle for the Bible.

When you deny the Word of God, you lose the Spirit of God, and when you lose the Spirit of God, you lose the power of God. That is how Satan effectively disarmed the Church in America. We have lost the sword of the Spirit, "which is the word of God" (Eph. 6:17).

> *The word of God is living and powerful, and sharper than any two-edged sword, piercing even to the division of soul and spirit, and of joints and marrow, and is a discerner of the thoughts and intents of the heart.*
> —HEBREWS 4:12

If you want to have victory against your most powerful adversary, you had better have confidence in your weaponry. And many are no longer going into war with their greatest weapon. Because we laid down the sword, the Church is now powerless to impact society morally or spiritually. Since we no longer believe in the authority of Scripture, who's to say who's right and who's wrong, what is right and what is wrong? So we sink deeper into Satan's snare of moral relativism. It is spiritual and moral anarchy. What is true of society may be just as true of your life personally. Satan wants to lead you into bondage and slavery.

We have an entire generation, most of whom claim to be Christian, but deny the authority of Scripture and thereby deny any moral or spiritual absolutes. We cannot agree on something as fundamental and simple as the definition of marriage. Hsssssssss.... "Has God really said what a marriage is...?" Hsssssssss... In Matthew 19:4-5,

Jesus defined marriage as between a man and a woman. Yet whole "Christian" denominations within the American "Church" have abandoned something as simple as the definition of marriage and the most basic issues of morality in human sexuality.

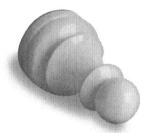

When you abandon the Bible as God's moral authority, it eventually leads to moral anarchy.

The way Satan attacked Eve is the way he attacks our society and how he attacks you on a daily basis. It begins very subtly by inducing doubt about the Word of God. Satan does not have to attack the Bible if he can establish doubt in your mind about the Bible. He does not have to disprove it—all he has to do is establish doubt, and then he has you right where he wants you.

I believe because you are reading this book and learning about the devices of a very real devil, you believe in the authority of the Bible. You believe the Bible is without error and God-breathed, line by line, from God through the pens of men. But simply being a Bible believer will do you no good if you are not a Bible obeyer. There are plenty of people who claim to believe it, but they just do not obey it. And because of that, they are soft targets for Satan.

More times than I can count in my years of pastoral counseling, I've heard this exact line: "I know what the Bible says, but…"; "I know what the Bible says about divorce, but…"; "I know what the Bible says about this relationship I am having with this other woman, but…". The moment you say "but," you are about to take the bait. When you take the bait of Satan, I can promise you are going to be bitten. When you fall for the strategy of Satan, you are going to feel the sting of sin. Obedience is your ultimate winning strategy over sin and Satan. If you know what the Bible says, don't rationalize with it. Don't argue about it. Just do it. Doubting God's Word leads to denying God's Word, which leads to disobeying God's Word, which leads to death. Just ask Eve.

In Genesis 2:16, God said to Adam and Eve, "Of every tree of the garden you may freely eat." Then here comes Satan in Genesis 3:1, casting doubt about what God had said. The serpent paraphrased God's Word from Genesis 2:16, leaving out the word "freely," and then Eve responds in Genesis 3:2 with the very same paraphrase. How subtle. It was just one word taken out of God's Word. It's the same word Satan has been trying to take out ever since. Satan hates the word "freely" because God's salvation is free (see Eph. 2:8-9). It's not earned by works. Yet he loves to frame God as the ultimate "taskmaster."

> *And the woman said to the serpent, "We may eat the fruit of the trees of the garden; but of the fruit of the tree which is in the midst of the garden,*

God has said, 'You shall not eat it, nor shall you touch it, lest you die.'"
—GENESIS 3:2-3

They both took out the word "freely," and then Eve added, "...nor shall you touch it." God did not say not to touch it; He said do not eat from it. Not only did she subtract from God's Word, she added to God's Word. Eve only had two verses in her entire Bible, and she could not even get that right. Finally, she used her own private interpretation of what God said.

Did her paraphrase get the thought across? Of course it did. Did she communicate the general idea of what God said? Of course she did. But does her paraphrase have the same force as the Word of God? Does it have the same sharpness as the Word of God? Absolutely not! Satan got her to doubt it, then she diluted it, and now it is just a short leap into the lap of outright denial.

"You will not surely die. For God knows that in the day you eat of it your eyes will be opened, and you will be like God, knowing good and evil."
—GENESIS 3:4-5

Satan knew what God had said, but he knew better than to come out of the gate with an all-out attack on what God had said. Eve would never have fallen for that. The counterfeiter is much too clever. He began with just a little doubt, just asking the question. Once Eve's defenses were lowered because of doubt, she diluted God's Word and then denied it. He set her up with lies, he distorted reality, and then she took the bait and denied God's word by planting a seed of doubt. It was just a little paraphrase here, a little addition there, a little subtraction here. God's Word was diluted and distorted, and Eve became easy prey. He "jabbed" at what God had said, and now he's ready to land the haymaker. The cross punch with the power to land the knockout!

SATAN'S HAYMAKER

Second Corinthians 10:3 tells us, "Though we walk in the flesh, we do not war according to the flesh." You do not fight spiritual battles with bullets or machetes, grenade launchers, or ballistic missiles. You fight spiritual powers with a greater power—the Word of God, the "sword of the Spirit" (Eph. 6:17). Paul says in Ephesians 6:14, "having girded your waist with truth," you are able to stand against the deception of the devil that deceives with lies and messes and meddles with your mind—which is what happens next in this battle of the ages:

> *So when the woman saw that the tree was good for food, that it was pleasant to the eyes, and a tree desirable to make one wise, she took of its fruit and ate.*
>
> —Genesis 3:6

Satan did not just get Eve to question the Word of God. *He got her to question the character of God.* Read between the lines. Remember there's always "more than meets the eye." She not only questioned if God's Word was true, she questioned if God's Word was good! In his most subtle and conniving way, Satan was saying, "You know Eve, if God really loved you, He would let you eat of that tree. Why would God withhold this from you, Eve? Maybe God is not really good. Maybe He is trying to keep something from you, Eve." He wanted to meddle with her mind and distort her thinking.

Satan perverted Eve's mind from thinking about God's provision to thinking about God's prohibition.

How many times have you done that? I know I have been guilty of doing the same thing more times than I can remember. Eve no longer thought about all the things she could do, she became obsessed in thinking about the one thing she'd been told not to do. Instead of focusing on what was right, she was now focused on her "rights."

First Satan disguised his appearance. Then he deceived with lies. Now he has completely distorted Eve's mind so she's doing some really stinkin' thinkin'. Her thinking had been completely distorted. The reality is that God was going to let Adam and Eve eat of the tree of the knowledge of good and evil in His own way, in His own time. He hadn't planted it in the Garden and told Adam and Eve not to eat from it just to tempt them and torment them. God created them to be like Him—full of the knowledge of good and evil but without sin. The problem lies in the fact that they gained that knowledge in their own way apart from God. Like many of us, they got that education through the "school of hard knocks." You may have gotten a lot of your knowledge that way too. Knowledge learned apart from God can become a lifetime of painful lessons learned.

The third step in Satan's attack is to distort our minds.

There was another tree in the Garden of Eden—the tree of life. God was going to let Adam and Eve eat from that tree as well. Had they passed the test and abstained from eating of the tree of knowledge of good and evil, they would have eaten of the tree of life and lived forever in perfection. And all of their offspring, you and me, would have been born in perfection instead of born in sin with Adam's fallen nature.

Eve took the bait knowing full well what God had said. She knew what God said, "but." "But why shouldn't I eat of this tree?" Eve questioning God is no different than so many others today who say, "I know what God says *but* why shouldn't I sleep with my boyfriend?" Or "I know what God says *but* why shouldn't I steal from the

IRS?" Or "I know what God says *but* why should I give my whole tithe?" The problem is not merely that sin and disobedience is bad. *The problem is that sin makes you dead.* "In the day that you eat of it you shall surely die" (Gen. 2:17).

Why can't I have that?

Why can't I eat that?

Why can't I watch that?

I do not know how many times in pastoral ministry I have heard that same sentiment from someone who has succumbed to Satan's stinkin' thinkin'. I'll be counseling with them and trying to encourage them from the Word of God when they say something like this: "I know it is wrong, but God wants me to be happy." "I know what the Bible says about the adulterous relationship I am in, but God wants me to be happy," or "I know what the Bible says about divorce, but God wants me to be happy." Their thinking is completely distorted. They are rationalizing their sin and convincing themselves their actions are not only okay, they are even something good—perhaps even of God. They have convinced themselves God is more concerned with their happiness than their holiness. If only they would commit to pursuing holiness, then they would find true happiness. Satan wants you to strive for happiness apart from holiness. That is exactly what he used to tempt Eve. She was more focused on her rights than her righteousness. She went for happiness and she lost holiness, and in the end, she was neither happy nor holy. So it is for so many of Adam's sons and Eve's daughters.

Oh, how Satan distorts one's mind. I met with a man who had left his wife for another woman. He wasn't even divorced before he moved in with his "affair." Let's just call it what God calls it—adultery. It's immorality and depravity. I was encouraging him to get right with God, repent of his sin, and go back to his wife when he interrupted me. He said, "Phil, did it ever occur to you that just maybe I am the answer to this woman's prayer?" I said, "What?" He went on to tell me, "Just the other day she told me she had prayed for months that a man like me would come into her life. I think I am the answer to her prayer." This man was totally serious. I thought to myself, "Are you crazy? Are you certifiably loony? Have you lost your mind?" The answer is yes, he had lost his mind. That is always what Satan wants to do. Satan had distorted his thinking. *The lies of the enemy had created in him a false reality.* He said, "And by the way Phil, we are going to church together too." What? Where did he get this from? Hssssssssssss... This man bought the lie, and he took the bait of Satan. It was that same old one-two punch. He attacked through lies and attracted through lust.

There is no weapon in the universe that can counter the lies of Satan, other than the truth of God's Word. It is our greatest defense, and our sword better be a sharp one! When you embrace the lie, you are no more than a breath away from taking the bait. The lie will lead to your version of the tree of knowledge of good and evil, that place where you are most vulnerable to temptation. When you take the bait, you will absolutely get bitten. So what do we do? We gird up the loins of our mind because that is where the battle rages.

> *Therefore gird up the loins of your mind, be sober, and rest your hope fully on the grace that is to be brought to you at the revelation of Jesus Christ.*
> —1 PETER 1:13

In Peter's day, a Roman soldier would "gird up his loins" as he prepared for battle. His clothing was a tunic type covering that came down to his knees. (Yes, even tough guys wore skirts back then.) These were the days before army fatigues. The tunic would come down to the soldier's knees encumbering his ability to move quickly with speed and agility. He would roll it up and tuck it into the belt he wore around his waist (his loins) as he prepared to go into battle so his legs could move freely. We might say today to "roll up your sleeves" as we prepare for work or in this case, war. Peter's message is clear. It's going to take lots of work as we prepare for war, so gird up the loins of your mind. Paul gives us the strategy to wage warfare:

> *For though we walk in the flesh, we do not war according to the flesh. For the weapons of our warfare are not carnal* [they're not physical] *but mighty in God for pulling down strongholds, casting down arguments and every high thing that exalts itself against the knowledge of God,*

> *bringing every thought into captivity to the obedience of Christ.*
>
> —2 Corinthians 10:3-5

 Whatever goes on between your ears will either strengthen you or weaken you.

Satan cannot read your mind. Unlike God, he is neither omnipresent (everywhere) or omniscient (all-knowing). While he (or more specifically one of his demonic powers or principalities) cannot read your thoughts, he very much wants to introduce thoughts into your mind. He loves to plant thoughts in your mind and then convince you that his thoughts are your thoughts. It's exactly what happened to Peter as he tried to convince Jesus not to go to the cross. Satan had planted those thoughts in Peter's mind, and Jesus called it out saying, "Get behind Me, Satan!"

Every time a lie is introduced to your mind, every time a wicked thought or an evil imagination is introduced in your mind, you have to immediately cast it out. Do not entertain it or toy with it. If you do, it will eventually become mental idolatry, and idolatry always leads to bondage and captivity. As soon as that wicked thought is cast out, it must be replaced with a God thought. You have to actively take captive every single thought so your thoughts line up with God's thoughts *because whoever or whatever controls your mind will control you.*

Jesus said, "You shall know the truth, and the truth shall make you free" (John 8:32). But the lies of the enemy will bring you into captivity. Every decision comes down to this one question: Whom will you believe?

CHAPTER 9

SATAN'S BAIT AND SWITCH

Finally my brethren, be strong in the Lord and in the power of His might. Put on the whole armor of God that you may be able to stand against the wiles [schemes] of the devil. For we do not wrestle against flesh and blood, but against principalities, against powers, against the rulers of the darkness of this age, against spiritual hosts of wickedness in the heavenly places.

—EPHESIANS 6:10-12

A few years ago, my family and I fell victim to a bait and switch. Our children were still young, and we wanted to take them to Disney World in Orlando, Florida, for a special family vacation. We had been solicited by a company selling vacations on the cheap. It sounded like a good deal. The first leg of our trip began at an Orlando resort. The first sign this trip might not be all that was promised came when we arrived at the resort and walked into our room. We were immediately met with the poignant odor of urine. The entire room reeked of it, from the carpet to the curtains to the mattresses and even the pillows. We found stains on the bed sheets. We got another room. That one reeked of cigarette smoke. My wife and I aren't smokers so we had been promised a nonsmoking room. Unfortunately, it was all they had left so we had to make a choice—cigarette smoke or sleep in a dried urine-soaked bed. We chose the smoke.

I realized then that just maybe I hadn't done enough "intelligence gathering" before booking the trip. Still, I was sure the trip would all be worth it for the cruise that we would embark on the second half of the week. We arrived with anticipation to the port in southern Florida where we would be taking off for the Bahamas. We had paid for a two-day cruise to the Bahamas and got it at a really great price. This was a first as neither my wife nor I had ever been on a cruise.

When we arrived at the port in southern Florida, we were looking at all the massive cruise ships wondering which of these great big bad boys was ours. And then I remember seeing this little ship coming in. Compared to all the other giant cruise liners it reminded me of "Tommy Tug Boat" (a cartoon my kids were fond of watching at the time). Somebody said, "That is your boat coming in." Compared to all the others, it looked like something in my kids' bathtub. I thought to myself, "Oh no, not again." Too late—we had already taken the bait. It was the result of an epic failure on our part to do the hard work of "intelligence gathering." We named our ship "Tommy Tug Boat" and sang "row, row, row your boat" all the way to the Bahamas.

Now, this bait and switch cost us a week out of our lives. But what if it cost you a decade or 20 years of your life? What if it took years off your life? Satan wants to pull a bait and switch on you that will cost you all of your life. Fortunately for you and me, with some intelligence gathering on our adversary from Genesis 3, we know Satan's M.O.

> *So when the woman saw that the tree was good for food, that it was pleasant to the eyes, and a tree desirable to make one wise, she took of its fruit and ate. She also gave to her husband with her, and he ate.*
>
> —GENESIS 3:6

The Apostle John warns us not to be taken in by the bait of Satan.

> *Do not love the world or the things in the world. If anyone loves the world, the love of the Father is not in him. For all that is in the world—the lust of the flesh, the lust of the eyes, and the pride of life—is not of the Father but is of the world.*
>
> —1 JOHN 2:15-17

All three elements of the bait of Satan are at work in Genesis 3:16. First of all, it was good for food; secondly, it was pleasant to the eyes; and thirdly, a tree desirable to make one wise.

BAIT NUMBER ONE: THE LUST OF THE FLESH

The woman saw that the tree was good for food...

The first way Eve was tempted was with the lust of the flesh—gratifying physical desires and the physical cravings of our bodies. Anything that you do for your body to gratify it outside of God's will is sin. The most obvious examples would be sexual gratification through immorality, drugs, alcohol, or perhaps food or nicotine. It is important to understand that Adam and Eve weren't hanging out in a little backyard garden. The Garden of Eden was 1,500 miles wide, with tens of thousands of trees from which Eve could freely eat. Nor was Eve hungry. She had more than enough quantity and variety to be satisfied. The temptation had nothing to do with need and everything to do with lust. She craved it because it looked good to the palate—and God had said not to eat it.

In Luke 4:3, Satan tempted Jesus with the "lust of the flesh" by appealing to Jesus to turn the stones into bread after he had been fasting for 40 days. In his humanity, Jesus was hungry but He did not give in to Satan's temptation for instant gratification. From Eve to Jesus, to you and me, Satan always uses the same strategy.

BAIT NUMBER TWO: THE LUST OF THE EYES

...it was pleasant to the eyes...

Lust is anything you long for that God says you cannot have or do because it is not good for you and will only bring you pain. It is "the tree" of temptation in your life.

There are countless examples of how people lust for money or material possessions. It is the personal desires of this world for material things more than spiritual and eternal things. Retailers and advertisers have become experts in appealing to the lust of the eyes to entice you into buying the next shiny object. Just walk through any mall—the lust of the eyes is everywhere. Just watch the commercials on TV (better yet, don't). It's all about making you want the newest and the coolest, even though the one you have is only a year old.

The lust of the eyes is anything you gaze on, anything you see that you begin to covet. It is not a sin to want something, until that something becomes an idol for you. You begin to worship it and long for it until it consumes your every thought. Eventually, you'll do anything to get it. That is what happened to Eve. First, she saw it was good for food, and then it was pleasant to the eyes. She began to gaze on it, and then she began to covet it.

In Luke 4:5-7, Satan tempted Jesus with the *lust of the eyes* by showing Him all the kingdoms of the world, saying, "If you will worship before me, all will be Yours." Note that Jesus did not correct Satan's claims to the kingdoms of this world. They were legally his, having been transferred back to him when Adam lost dominion by succumbing to Satan's temptation. But unlike Eve, Jesus refused the instant gratification offered by Satan. You see, Jesus knew if He waited for God's timing and God's way, eventually those kingdoms would rightfully become His. And they will be one day soon.

BAIT NUMBER THREE: THE PRIDE OF LIFE

...desirable to make one wise...

The third category of the bait of Satan is the insatiable lust for power and prestige, self-pride, self-promotion, and the all-consuming desire to be esteemed among men. Genesis 3:6 records that it was *a tree desirable to make one wise.* Eve wanted to be esteemed. She wanted to promote herself. She was tempted because Satan had said this tree can make you "like God" (v. 5). She wanted the exact same thing that was Satan's downfall—to be like God. The irony is she already was. By this time her mind was completely distorted by Satan's deception. The lie of the enemy had become her false reality—that somehow she was insufficient and what God had given her was not enough.

In Luke 4:9-10, the devil used the very same tactic on Jesus, tempting Him with the *pride of life.* He told Jesus to throw Himself off the pinnacle of the temple to *prove* He was the Son of God. He even contorted and twisted the Scripture, saying, "For it is written: 'He shall give His angels charge over you, to keep you.'" He was tempting Jesus to prove He was really the Messiah by putting His very life in such peril the angels would come and catch Him. He was tempting Jesus to lift Himself up, outside the will of God, simply to prove He was the Son of God. But unlike the first Adam, the last Adam wouldn't take the bait. He was secure in His identity and had nothing He needed to prove to this counterfeit king.

Satan's scheme worked like a charm on Eve—but not on Jesus, because He was unlike any other man Satan had ever encountered. Jesus was the eternal, sinless Son of God, the virgin-born Son. Because He was virgin-born, He had no earthly father. Because He had no earthly father, He did not have Adam's fallen nature or his fallen image. He only had the nature of His heavenly Father, which is holy.

Satan's method against Eve and against Jesus is the same method he uses against you and me. He wants to bait you and tempt you because sin always brings death and destruction (see Rom. 6:23). Sin will bring death to your relationships, death to your home, death to your marriage. It will bring death to your wealth and death to your health. Don't take Satan's bait!

I know a little about baiting traps because I live in the country. When you live in the country, you have mice. I have learned to hate mice. I have personally declared war on mice. I don't care what the PETA people think of me. For me, the only good mouse is a dead mouse! I think they must be part of God's curse on Adam's sin. (Okay, that's silly theology but you get the point.) Besides being nasty little vermin, they chew through everything. They have destroyed the wiring in my tractor. They have built their nests in the engine compartment of my lawn mower. They have cost me time and money. As you can see, I don't like mice.

The common tactic to kill and destroy a mouse is a little like the way Satan baits us. You set a mouse-trap with a piece of cheese on it. Then here comes the mouse looking for something to satisfy his appetite. Not too long ago, I saw evidence of a mouse in the house. I set the trap and baited it. I then went into a different room of the house where I could sit and watch the trap. A few minutes later, I saw a mouse emerge from around the corner. He immediately approached the trap. I could almost see what he was thinking, "It looks so good but I know I shouldn't do it. I know it's dangerous. I'll just get close enough to sniff it." He quickly darted away from the trap. He knew it didn't look right. He knew he needed to be cautious, but he just couldn't stay away.

A minute later he was back. Same sniff test. Same reaction. He quickly darted away. He somehow knew he shouldn't take the bait. I got up and started doing some-thing else, but a few minutes later I heard the metallic *snap*! One dead mouse. One has to wonder what the last thought was that crossed his little mind. "I know I shouldn't do it but I just can't help it! It smells so good… it looks so good! I'll just go for one quick bite…." Okay maybe mice can't actually process that well, but you get the point. He knew it was extremely dangerous, but he chose to risk his life to take the bait.

I hate to admit it, but even though I've got a mind a little better than a mouse, at times in my life I have taken

Satan's bait. Satan knows the bait we're most apt to take. And taking the bait will always bring death. Romans 6:23 says, "The wages of sin is death...." Yes, death eternally and death spiritually, but so much more. It will bring death to life's joy, your family, your friendships, your marriage, your future, your children, your finances, your wealth, your health. It may be years in the making, but eventually, the wages of sin is always death! If you've been born again by faith in the shed blood of Jesus, your sin cannot destroy your salvation because your salvation is built on Christ's work and not your work. But sin can destroy everything else.

That is exactly how it ended for Adam and Eve.

> *Then the eyes of both of them were opened, and they knew that they were naked; and they sewed fig leaves together and made themselves coverings.*
> —GENESIS 3:7

Sin always brings shame, and the first thing they wanted to do was cover up the parts of themselves that gave them shame. Proverbs 28:13 says, "He who covers his sins will not prosper. But whoever confesses and forsakes them will have mercy." The first thing to do if you are caught in the bait of Satan is to quit the cover-up so Jesus can start the clean-up. But the first thing Adam and Eve did was find a hideout for their cover-up.

Genesis 3:8 tells us, "They heard the sound of the Lord God walking in the garden in the cool of the day, and Adam and his wife hid themselves from the presence of the Lord God among the trees of the garden."

Sin not only alienated them from each other, it caused them to isolate themselves from God as well. Sin can only bring alienation and isolation. It makes you want to hide from God because God is holy.

> *Then the Lord God called to Adam and said to him, "Where are you?"*
> —GENESIS 3:9

God hadn't lost Adam, He knows everything. He wasn't walking in the Garden saying, "Come out, come out wherever you are!" God wanted Adam to come out from hiding on his own. If you are caught in Satan's bait of sin, that is how you deal with it. You come out from hiding, you quit running, you quit covering up, and you say, "God, here I am, and boy did I blow it."

> *So he said, "I heard Your voice in the garden, and I was afraid because I was naked; and I hid myself." And He said, "Who told you that you were naked? Have you eaten from the tree of which I commanded you that you should not eat?"*
> —GENESIS 3:10, 11

God is omniscient. He knew what Adam had done. Just like a parent knows what little five-year-old Johnny has done when you tell him, "Don't touch the vase on the coffee table," and then you leave the room and the next thing you hear is the vase shattering. You come back in and say to little Johnny, "What have you done!?" You know what little Johnny has done. What you want is for him to admit what he has done. You want him to take ownership for what he has done, just as God wanted Adam to get to a place of ownership and responsibility so there could be repentance and restoration.

God hates sin because it is the source of all human suffering. God never intended human beings to ever suffer. Before Adam's sin, everything was in perfection and all was perfect in creation. It was a perfect place, a perfect planet. We were perfect people with a perfect God. Everything was absolutely perfect until sin entered creation and sent all creation into chaos. And suddenly there was isolation, alienation, death, and destruction.

All suffering is because of sin.

The entire universe is built on the law of "cause and effect." When it comes to human suffering, sin is the cause and suffering is the effect. Cancer, Alzheimer's, diabetes—all disease is the curse of Adam's sin. All of your suffering is because of either Adam's sin, somebody else's sin, or your sin. Now you can see why God hates sin because it always leads to suffering. And this is what God wants you to understand. While Satan cannot destroy your salvation because it has been bought by the Son and sealed by the Spirit, he can destroy everything else. Satan wants to lead you back into captivity and slavery, even though Jesus has given you a position of power, authority, liberty, and victory.

That is why Paul says, do not "give place to the devil" (Ephesians 4:27). That little verse tucked away in the Book of Ephesians is so important because as the redeemed of God, the devil has lost his place in your life. He has no authority over your life, and he has no place in your life. But every single time you sin, you give him back a little place again. And when you sin over and over again in the same area of your life, you are giving him back authority over that area of your life.

When you sin, it gives Satan a toehold. Do it again and again, and the toehold becomes a foothold; do it some more, and the foothold becomes what the Bible calls a stronghold. A stronghold is an area of your life you have failed to submit to the authority of Jesus Christ. You have given Satan back authority over that area of your life. His desire is simply to lead you progressively, step by step, from a place of liberty to a place of captivity.

If I tied the hands of even an average man behind his back with a single strand of thin string, it would in no way hold him in bondage. He could easily break free. One sin is like one piece of string. Satan cannot hold you in bondage with just one sin, but that one sin leads to another sin. Every time you keep sinning over and over again in that same area, Satan wraps another string around you until—like wrapping string after string around that man's wrists—you cannot possibly break free.

Sin is the bait Satan uses to ensnare us and enslave us.

No alcoholic was born an alcoholic. He took just one drink, just one string, and did it one too many times. He realized the alcohol helped relieve the stress, the strain, and the pain of life. But the relief was only temporary, so he had to reach for another drink and then another, day after day, and then another. Pretty soon he was no longer reaching for the drink, the drink was reaching for him. It had become a stronghold in his life. He was no longer living in liberty—but captivity.

No grade school girl grows up thinking, "I can't wait to be old enough to finally have sex with so many different guys that I can get that reputation of being the 'easy' girl in school." No, that's not how it happens. But Satan knows how it happens. He knows in the heart of every young lady the deepest need she has is to feel beautiful and special. So he convinces her she is not beautiful; she is not special. Perhaps her father never told her she was special. He never treated her like his "Cinderella." Maybe her older sister was the Homecoming Queen and voted best looking in her Senior Class—and it felt like she could never measure up. Maybe someone made fun of her acne when she was in the 8th grade. Maybe when she looked in the mirror, she didn't see the perfect body she sees on television, and she thought, "I'm not enough." That is the lie of the enemy. Hssssssss...

She learns early in life she can feel beautiful and special by dressing provocatively and sensually because when she does, boys give her the attention and the kind of affirmation that makes her feel beautiful and special. Then she learns she can feel more beautiful and more special by turning to sex because when she has sex with them, boys give her even more attention—lots and lots of attention! And it makes her feel more beautiful and more special—temporarily. But the feeling is not lasting. So she gives her body away again and again—until ten or twenty years later, sex feels more like a prison. Her life is full of pain and her heart full of shame. And it all began when she believed the lie and took the bait. She was already beautiful. She was already special. God says so, and since He's the one who made her, He ought to know.

Sin is a counterfeit and a false solution to life's problems. Only God can really make someone feel special or beautiful. Our worth comes from Him and not another.

Sin is an attempt to meet a God-given need in an ungodly way. It's a longing for intimacy that turns into marital infidelity. It's temporarily exciting and gratifying. Someone confuses intensity with intimacy, and Satan lures them into captivity. It's the same old one-two combination he threw at Eve. He jabs with the lie and throws the knockout with lust.

All sin is someone's attempt to meet a legitimate need in an illegitimate way.

While God has put in the heart of women the need to feel beautiful and the need to feel special, God has put in the hearts of men the need to feel strong and the need to feel powerful. Satan knows if he can convince a young man that he is not strong and significant, that he is actually rather weak, the young man is apt to take any bait. Maybe it began when he was only a grade-schooler, mercilessly bullied by his older brother and repeatedly called a "sissy" or worse. Maybe he landed hard after his first girlfriend broke up with him for a more handsome upperclassman. "Am I not handsome enough? Am I not good enough?" Maybe he never got picked to be on the best team in school. Maybe all he ever heard from his father was, "You're a born loser…you'll never amount to anything." Somewhere along the way, he began to believe a lie that said, "I am not enough. I can never measure up. I don't really have what it takes." Do you hear the serpent's hsssssssssss…?

What does a young man do when God has made him to feel strong but he actually feels weak? He might turn to work and become a workaholic. Or he might turn to women and become a sex addict. Having sex makes him feel strong and significant. Yes, it's physically gratifying, but what drives him really is how it makes him feel about his masculinity—like he's "da man." So his life becomes one of endless *conquest*. He's all about the "score." He lusts for women's attention as much as he lusts for their bodies. He needs their affirmation to make him feel masculine. It makes him feel *strong* and *significant.* The ultimate stroke to his broken male ego is when he has sex. That's where he can really prove to himself he's a man. Every time he pursues a woman and she gives in, it fills him with a sense of strength and significance masking his insecurity over his broken masculinity. He's not aware of it. Satan conceals it from him. He doesn't understand what is really driving him. But he's broken.

Sometimes it happens when he is still a teenager, and he turns to this counterfeit love and attention instead of Christ. A man's strength comes from God and his identity is in Christ. Yet even when he becomes an adult, sometimes even after years of marriage, he still turns to sex to fill the gaping hole in his heart. It's a hole too large for any one woman to fill. So now he's a "repeater cheater." Satan knows what sexual addiction is made of. And this guy is an addict. Sex is for him what cocaine is for another. Until this man is set free by Jesus, he will continue making "conquests" into his old age. His life is one of secrecy in an effort to fill his broken masculinity. He's so full of insecurity, having never understood his true identity. Now he's in slavery to pornography or adultery, and his whole life is one big merry-go-round of sensuality. It is a captivity from which he cannot escape on his own, and it all began when he believed the lies of the enemy. *He was strong all along! He was significant already!* God has put strength in all of Adam's sons. God said so and He should know.

Pornography is a cancer in our society and a counterfeit solution to a man's longing for intimacy. Pornography is one of the reasons we are becoming a nation of sexual predators, perverts, and prisoners. There is an epidemic of young men in our society still in their twenties who ought to be in the prime of their sexual energy but they must rely on products like Viagra just to function properly. Their minds no longer work properly because thousands of sexual images have altered and confused the chemical reactors in the brain that tell the body what to do. It's why Paul wrote 2000 years ago, before medical science could have been fully understood, to "Flee sexual immorality. Every sin that a man does is outside the body, but he who commits sexual immorality sins against his own body" (1 Cor. 6:18). Sexual sin literally changes the brain on the cellular level. Satan knows this. And he knows all too well that a man's sexuality is how God made him to bond emotionally and connect intimately with a woman. Having sex for a man is easy, but sexual intimacy can sometimes be difficult and full of disappointment. Satan offers a counterfeit and a shortcut. When a man clicks on pornography, it is completely safe. It is totally controlled, and the end is never in doubt. He knows he is going to get it in the "end zone" every time, but the "fix" is temporary. The problem is…the feeling is oh so fleeting. So he finds himself going back again and again and again to that same polluted, poisonous well.

So Satan keeps wrapping that string over and over again around this man's soul until he has slowly led him from a place of liberty back into captivity. Not unlike his fallen father Adam, he has now given back dominion to Satan. He believed the lie and took the bait. And that bait has become his bondage. But the good news is it's not too late for him. He can win against sin.

PART III

YOU CAN WIN

But thanks be to God, who gives us the victory through
our Lord Jesus Christ.
—1 CORINTHIANS 15:57

Battles are won or lost before they are ever fought. When I was on the SWAT team, we prepared for the time when we might find ourselves in a fight for our very lives. We spent hours and hours in training and repetition after repetition so when the moment of truth finally arrived, our response would be second nature. It's too late to think about what to do in the heat of battle. Battles are won long before they are ever fought. If you wait to prepare when the bullets start flying, it's too late. We would draw our weapons over and over without ever firing a shot. Our weapons needed to become an extension of our bodies. Drawing your weapon smoothly and quickly needed to be as second nature as walking and talking—not something you have to think about doing. We shot thousands of rounds through our weapons. When your life is on the line, you better make a good shot. You don't have a lot of time to aim and finally pull the trigger. The bad guy isn't pondering whether he should shoot you or not. His mind is made up, and he's trying to shoot you.

We would make entry after entry on empty houses and buildings over and over again, learning how to move quietly and safely as a unit. Everyone had to know exactly what to do without any further instruction. Everybody had a different job to do, and we had to do it together. If we didn't, someone could get shot. Hours and hours and weeks and weeks and months and months we trained until our job became second nature without having to think about it. And then it finally happened...

The time came one night without warning. That is always how Satan attacks. He doesn't call ahead and he doesn't give us a heads-up to let us know he's coming. You just have to be ready, as Peter told us in First Peter 5:8 to "be sober, be vigilant."

It was a hot and humid August night back in 1997. Our shift was almost over when the call came in. A man, estranged from his wife, had taken the woman hostage after pistol whipping her in the front yard of their home. The neighbors were mortified. As he was beating her about the head with his gun—it went off. His wife's head was bleeding profusely. The horrified neighbors thought he'd shot her in the head before dragging her inside the house. Negotiations broke down. The bad guy was threatening a murder–suicide. He swore he was going to kill her and then kill himself. We had no other option. We were going in.

As we opened the front door, the bullets started flying. If you have ever been in a life and death situation, you know it's an out-of-body experience. The sound of gunfire became muffled, and what took only seconds seemed to be taking place in slow motion. The husband tried to bait us into going up the staircase to get him where he had an elevated position from which to shoot us. Because of our training, we immediately knew not to take the bait! No way were we going up that "fatal funnel," as we called it. When we wouldn't go up the stairs, the man came down firing. I don't mean to sound at all cavalier, but that was the last mistake he would ever make. Our training took over, and the entire ordeal ended in a matter of seconds. No one had time to think about what to do, nor did anyone need to take a minute to think it over. Our response was automatic. We saved the woman's life while the bad guy lost his. None of our guys were hit. We did exactly what we were trained to do. The hours and hours of training had paid off.

Most Christians aren't prepared for the heat of battle. If you have to think about what to do, it's too late. Your weapon (God's Word) has to be an extension of your being. Your body armor (your faith) has to already be in place. Your mind has to be trained how to react correctly ahead of time. In SWAT training, we call it "muscle memory." Something that comes so naturally you don't think about it. As Christians, we must develop a "spiritual memory" that is finely tuned to detect and deflect the enemy's advances. The average Christian is woefully unprepared, having never gone through the repetition of really knowing how to win. So they continue over and over again to live in a prison when they don't have to, repeating the same mistakes. All of that can change when you make the decision ahead of time not to take the bait.

You are not Jesus, but if you have been born again, the Spirit of the Living God lives inside of you. That means you are not "the" Son of God, but you are "a" son of God or you are "a" daughter of God. That means you can win against sin. Jesus said in John 8:36, "If the Son makes you free, you shall be free indeed." He is trying to tell you that you can trade captivity for liberty, victory instead of slavery.

Your greatest defense against the wiles of the adversary is to follow Jesus' example. In Matthew 4, He was tempted by the devil in the very same way Eve was tempted. Three times He countered Satan's lies with the truth of what God had said. Three times He was tempted, and three times He whipped out His sword and said, "It is written...It is written...It is written." And with three precise strikes from the Word of God, He cut His enemy to shreds. He did not paraphrase, He did not leave anything out, and He did not add His own personal interpretation. He simply stood on what God had said.

Your defense is the difference between what Jesus did and Eve did not do. Jesus stood on what God had said. When you understand the Word of God and know how to use it, you have a weapon that is more powerful than any weapon in the universe.

CHAPTER 10

DON'T TAKE THE BAIT!

The bait of Satan is not always as sinister sounding as cocaine or pornography. It's sometimes very subtle and sounds far more "acceptable." Comfort food brings comfort. The food itself is not a sin, but when it replaces Jesus as our source of comfort, it becomes an idol. Money is not immoral, and having lots of it is not sinful. Money is a necessity, but when it becomes your source of security, it too becomes idolatry. *All idolatry eventually leads to our captivity.* You can see why Paul would write in First Corinthians 10:14, "Therefore, my beloved, flee from idolatry." What cocaine is for one person, shopping can become to another. The same bondage found in alcohol for the alcoholic is the same bondage found in work for the workaholic. Satan doesn't only use things that are "evil." He relishes in taking something God intended for good and turning it into something evil to use against us. Whether or not you have been conducting intelligence gathering on Satan, you can rest assured he has been doing some intelligence gathering on you. He knows the bait you are most apt to take, *and that bait will become your source of bondage!*

The bait of Satan is directly related to our brokenness.

Our area of captivity is directly related to a lie from the enemy. Every lie he sows in us is somehow related to the same lie he planted in Eve's heart—"God is not suffi-cient and God is not enough." Satan knows if he can get us to believe that lie, we will always find another "god."

Satan knows our areas of brokenness and custom-makes the bait for each of his victims. Looking back on my adoles-cence and early years as a very young man, I know now what drove me was my own broken identity and sense of masculinity. I didn't have the knowledge or maturity to self-diagnose what was driving my decisions as I do now. Looking back, I was that young man who longed to feel strong and powerful but inwardly felt weak. I was that young man full of insecurity, always questioning if any woman would find me desirable. "Will anyone ever really love me? Am I handsome enough? Am I strong enough?"

I masked it well. I learned to turn to athletics for my affirmation and need for attention. Nobody who knew me would have ever suspected the level of loneliness and insecurity I lived with day in and day out. I was the school jock with lots of friends. I was the kid walking around the high school campus with all the patches on his letter jacket, with plenty of awards and recognition. I started on the varsity football team as a sophomore and my name was constantly being blared through the speaker system, heard by hundreds every Friday night. I enjoyed waking up the next day and seeing my name on the Saturday morning sports page of the local newspaper. But it was never enough to numb the growing emptiness inside.

I was slowly succumbing to Satan's lie that said, "I wasn't strong. I wasn't enough. I would never measure up. No woman will ever want me. No one will ever love me. You don't have what it takes to make a woman happy." I was still just a kid when it started. That's when it begins for all of us because Satan knows when we are most vulnerable. He strikes while we're still young. *The lies of the enemy begin shaping our broken identity that will eventually define our destiny.* He was hard at work, trying to define mine.

I started dating while still in middle school. I tell parents today that letting your kids date and pursue romantic relationships at too young an age will only end in temptation, frustration, drama, and trauma. We think these teeny bopper relationships are just fun and part of growing up. I beg to differ. Our cultural method of randomly dating, hoping to eventually stumble onto the "one" is the reason so many stand at the altar to take their vows with a completely unhealthy heart, full of brokenness. We call it baggage, and we wonder why there are so many unhealthy marriages. It's because there are a lot of unhealthy people. It all began while they were still children at heart. Disobedience while dating breeds dysfunction in marriage. The same dysfunctional patterns you set in motion as a single, will carry into your marriage. I should know.

I was still in junior high and not remotely prepared for the trap Satan had set for me one afternoon on the back of a school bus. I was sitting next to a girl I really liked, and she liked me too. All I can say is that something happened on the back of that bus that I wasn't looking for that day. It was something I didn't initiate and something I didn't even know existed. I lost my innocence that day. Something was awakened that should have stayed asleep for another ten years, and I struggled with sexual lust from that day forward until Jesus set me free years later.

I began pursuing girls. I got dumped after six months by the first girl I ever really liked and I landed really hard. You might say I landed and something shattered—my heart. I was so heartsick that I actually stayed home from school. "How could she do this to me? She said she loved me! Why am I not good enough for her? What did I do wrong?" The truth is I hadn't done anything wrong, and honestly, she hadn't either. We were both just kids playing grown-up games with feelings and emotions we didn't know how to handle. Satan used that to begin sowing in me a lie of my inadequacy.

It was the first time in my life I felt the sting of rejection. I received a *soul wound* that would deeply affect my life. God has put a longing in our hearts for love and acceptance. How did I deal with that pain? The only way I knew how. I eventually found another girl—prettier than the first. Yeah…I'll show her I have what it takes! And it worked…for a few months. Then it too fizzled. Not to worry. It's my sophomore year of high school and I am the "sophomore sensation" varsity football player. I caught the attention of a very pretty girl. "Wow…now she really likes me. Look at how she smiles when she sees me coming!" Finally, I was feeling good about who I was. "Maybe I really am enough of a man to make a woman happy." I didn't have the maturity then to really think in those terms, but now I understand what was driving me. Instead of looking to Jesus, I was looking to girls to establish my masculinity. "Mirror, mirror on the wall, do you find me acceptable and desirable at all?" And this girl said "Yes"! She made me feel like "da man"! It was great while it lasted. But in a few months football season was over…and I got dumped for a wrestler.

I am actually smiling as I recount this story. It seems rather silly now, perhaps even a little funny. Those wounds healed many years ago. But at that tender age, there was nothing funny about it. Truthfully, that is how it begins for many men who years later are asking themselves, "Am I enough of a man?" Have you ever wondered why some men throw away great marriages and shatter their families by running off with a younger woman? It's not because of what the younger woman looks like. It's because of what she makes him feel like! How many stories do you hear about men at the pinnacle of success in their ministry, business, position in government, or another high-end profession who get caught in a sex scandal and suddenly lose it all? Let me tell you why they were willing to jeopardize and risk so much: inwardly they are still that teenage boy full of insecurity asking themselves that same question, "Am I enough of a man?"

I understand what drives them to make the most irrational decisions because I know now that it could have been me. *They're not searching for sex. They're searching for significance.* I didn't know it then, but I was looking for my identity that was all the while being shaped through the lies of the enemy. It was one failed relationship after another after another. Satan, whose name means accuser, was there the entire time accusing me saying, "You're not enough." It's not that girls didn't like me. Lots of them did. Just not the ones I liked.

By the time I left high school for the University of Kansas with a full-ride football scholarship, I had fully embraced Satan's lies and taken his bait—hook, line, and sinker! Though I was living the "dream" playing Division 1 football, I was headed down a destructive pattern that, but for the grace of God, would have led to sexual addiction and maybe alcoholism as well. I found that by drinking, I was more acceptable. I was the life of the party—the "good time" guy! So I drank, and drank a lot. Alcoholism, promiscuity, marital infidelity, pornography! Who knows where my life might have gone had Jesus not radically intercepted my life at the age of 21? What I do know now is I lusted for the attention of women. I needed the affirmation of women. By this time in my life, I was getting lots of attention, and I'd learned how to get more. That is the beginning of sexual addiction. It is not so much about the sex but rather the emotional fix.

Every time I would reel a girl in, it would stroke my broken male ego. It would temporarily answer the nagging question in my sinful broken heart with, "Yes, I do have what it takes. I am desirable. I am enough of a man." I wish I could say what saved me from a life of promiscuity was my love for Jesus, but that wouldn't be true. At this time in my life, I was far from God. The truth is it was my love for a girl I had met in English class my senior year of high school that kept me from "sleeping around." I wanted to eventually marry her, and I didn't want to mess that up. Sadly, I didn't have to have sex with other girls for them to fill my broken heart; just knowing that I could was enough.

Take inventory of your life. Ask Jesus to reveal the source of the brokenness in your heart.

Jesus said in Luke 4:18, "He has sent Me to heal the brokenhearted" and that is exactly what I needed. I married that beautiful girl from my English class. Christa was my dream girl, voted best looking of our senior class. She was the girl all the guys wanted, and I'm the one who married her! Little did I know she could not heal my wounded heart. Only Jesus could do that. As I shared earlier, disobedience in dating will lead to dysfunction in marriage. After years of marriage, ours was becoming increasingly dysfunctional. By now, I had been a member of KC SWAT and had received lots of awards and recognition. I had been promoted to supervisor, one of the youngest sergeants on the department. I was one of the department's up-and-comers. I had the respect of my peers and success in my work, but I knew I was failing my wife. By this time, my commitment to Christ was more than enough to keep me faithful to the marriage vows I'd taken, shunning the women who "hit" on the uniform. But my marriage was in decline and looking back, it was less about Christa and far more about me. The truth is she too had broken my heart along the way. I had pursued her, but I deeply wanted her to pursue me.

Jesus intercepted me at the age of 21 and radically changed the trajectory of my life. I quit drinking altogether and soon quit chasing girls. But there is a vast difference between being forgiven of your sin and being healed from your sin.

There is a vast difference between being forgiven of your sin and being healed from your sin.

Isaiah 53:5 tells us that "by His [Jesus] stripes we are healed." Jesus came to forgive us AND to heal us. I'd been forgiven, but still needed to be healed. At the time I didn't know the difference, and I had no idea what I needed. I had brought all those same insecurities and broken masculinity into my marriage. As the years wore on, they would emerge more and more often. My wife would hurt me by something she would say or do. It was usually unintentional, but something would hit my trigger. I never thought about it consciously, but I now know deep down I wondered if Christa marrying me was a "fluke"—that one day she would wake up and realize she'd made a huge mistake. She would realize I wasn't good enough for her and dump me just like all the others. The lie of the enemy that had formed a false reality in me years earlier was becoming a self-fulfilling prophecy.

A man will mask his insecurity and feelings of being weak in relation to a woman in one of two ways: by blowing up and getting angry or retreating inwardly emotionally. Sometimes I would blow up, but most of the time I would retreat. I might not talk to my wife for three or four days. It was my way of taking back my manhood. A man will do anything to protect it. Of course, it didn't work because what I really wanted was for her to pursue me the way I had pursued her. But a man is never less desirable to a woman than when he stops talking to her. Worse yet, while I was dying on the inside, I didn't realize that my selfish actions were slowly killing her. One night I heard her crying in the darkness of the night. I heard the Spirit of God whisper deep inside me, "If you don't take care of her, you could lose her." I was instantly broken. It wasn't the brokenness of my youth. This was the brokenness that brings true healing. I had withheld a portion of my heart for many years. I'd withheld it from God, and I'd withheld it from my wife. I had learned along the way that I couldn't trust anybody with my heart, and I needed to protect it. That night I relinquished it. All my married life I had tried to protect myself from pain. But for the first time, I learned what it really meant to love your wife as Christ loved the Church (see Eph. 5:25). That night I chose the nails.

Over the next weeks and months, God showed me my heart and revealed things I had long ago forgotten— things I'd buried for years beneath the surface of my outward success and SWAT cop persona. I recognized the lies I believed and the bait I had taken. I recognized the *soul wounds* I had received that Satan had leveraged to his advantage. And Jesus did exactly what He promised—by His stripes I was healed.

What lies have you believed that could be holding you captive?

When we believe a lie from the enemy, idolatry begins to form in us. An idol is a false god we begin serving when we should be serving God. And idolatry always leads to captivity. Our area of brokenness leads to the bait, and the bait becomes our bondage. Do not ever forget...Satan knows your area of brokenness and crafts the lies and the bait accordingly.

Why do some people become workaholics? I know a fellow pastor who one day overheard his secretary on the phone having a conversation. He didn't know who she was talking to but he heard her say, "Well you know our pastor is not a very good preacher, but he sure does work hard." That comment was a wound on his soul. It cut him to the core. A man longs to feel strong and significant. That comment made him feel weak and inadequate. From that day forward, he determined to outwork everyone he knew. He would prove he had what it took to be a success. If he couldn't succeed in his preaching, he would succeed in whatever way he could. He was always the first one in the office in the morning and the last one to leave in the evening. This went on for years, and it almost cost him his family. The lies of the enemy always create in us a false reality. He was already a success because He was serving Jesus—there was nothing else he needed to prove.

I know of a man who struggled with his weight all of his life. He was obese. He had a food addiction that began years earlier when he was just a little boy. Deep down, he knew his older brother was his father's favorite. His father always bragged on his older brother for his ability in sports. But unlike his older brother, he was not very athletic, and he never heard his father's affirming words. He longed for his dad to be as proud of him as he was of his older brother. He knew his father wasn't proud of him, and it became a wound on his soul. One night at the dinner table he ate everything on his plate. He was still hungry so he ate the leftovers from his brother's plate. For the first time, he heard his father's affirming words, "Wow! Look at that boy eat. He sure can put away the groceries!" He had finally accomplished what every little boy longs to do—he had made his father proud. From that day forward, he ate everything on his plate and anything left on anybody else's too. That habit became a food addiction, and it all began with a wound that was inflicted upon his soul.

Do you see how subtle Satan is? Something that seems so insignificant can be the very thing Satan uses to begin forming in us a lie that we believe. The lie we believe forms the bait we take. We are driven by a false reality, and that lie of the enemy becomes the source of our captivity. Even religion itself can become the deception of the enemy to lead us into captivity. Jesus didn't come to give us "religion," He came to give us "redemption." Religion is something we do for God, but redemption is something God does for us. Satan convinces us we can earn God's love and God's favor by the religious or righteous things we do. *Religion is just another one of Satan's prisons.* If that is how we must earn God's acceptance, how will we ever know when we have finally done enough? Who convinced you that you had to earn God's love? Hsssssssssss... The truth is as a child of God, you already have God's love. If it could be earned, it wouldn't be love.

I want to encourage you to take a fearless and searching inventory of your life to discover if there is a stronghold in any part of your life—that besetting sin— that sin that ensnares you again and again. Ask yourself, "What is the area in my life where I am not completely free? Where am I not living in the victory Jesus won for me at Calvary?" As a born-again, blood-bought child of God, you have already been forgiven. But you can also be free.

CHAPTER 11

IDENTITY CRISIS

Then Jesus said to those Jews who believed Him, "If you abide in My word, you are My disciples indeed. And you shall know the truth, and the truth shall make you free."
—JOHN 8:31-32

Jesus answered them, "Most assuredly, I say to you, whoever commits sin is a slave of sin. And a slave does not abide in the house forever, but a son abides forever. Therefore if the Son makes you free, you shall be free indeed."
—JOHN 8:34-36

The implication Jesus was making is clear. As the fallen sons of Adam and the fallen daughters of Eve, we are born in captivity. It's true of us all. Our physical father

Adam sold us all into slavery under Satan's dominion and authority. But at the moment we put our faith in the shed blood of Jesus and trust Him to forgive our sin, we are instantly redeemed from Satan's authority and sin's penalty. Colossians 1:13 says, God "has delivered us from the power of darkness and conveyed us into the kingdom of the Son of His love." As Christians, God has placed us in Christ, and our positional reality is one of ultimate freedom in Christ. We are free from the penalty of sin and free from Satan's dominion. Your true identity as a blood-bought child of God is blameless and spotless, triumphant and victorious. *Your identity is no longer in the sinful things you have done but rather what Christ did on the cross.* Sin is not your master because Jesus has set you free.

Freedom, however, is not always our practical reality. Many never experience this liberty experientially. Practically, we can continue living for years like we're in captivity long after Jesus has set us free to live life abundantly. One of the darkest chapters in our nation's history is slavery. What a testament to human depravity that one man would forcibly enslave another. Yet it went on for centuries in the western hemisphere until it was finally banned by Great Britain and eventually the United States. Sadly, it continues even today in many parts of the world. As you know, it was finally ended in our nation by a bloody Civil War where over five hundred thousand Americans lost their lives. What a tragic chapter in our nation's history.

What happened after the war was over is just as bad. The institution of slavery was forever legally banned in the United States by the signing of the 13th Amendment to the U.S. Constitution passed by Congress on January 31, 1865, and ratified on December 6, 1865. On December 7, 1865, legally there were no slaves anywhere in the United States. None. Legally, all slaves were set free. They were free to leave their old masters, and no one could legally stop them. They were free to go wherever they wanted. Yet many of them stayed. Many of them continued living as though they were still a slave. Why did they stay when they could have walked away? Because many of them were never told they had been set free. Their old masters lied to them about the truth. Their old masters concealed the truth and distorted the truth. Does that sound at all familiar in light of all we've learned?

Our old master is a liar and seeks to hide the truth from us. He wants to convince us we are still slaves to sin and under his dominion, when we have legally been set free to serve a new Master. That new Master beckons us all saying, "Come to Me, all you who labor and are heavy laden, and I will give you rest. Take My yoke upon you and learn from Me, for I am gentle and lowly in heart, and you will find rest for your souls. For My yoke is easy and My burden is light" (Matt. 11:28-30). Unlike our old master, our new Master is not a cruel taskmaster. When we were yoked to Satan, it was a life of slavery and captivity. But now that we are yoked to Christ, He promises a life of freedom and liberty.

Yet many still live in that same old prison of addiction, depression, alcoholism, or some other pattern of dysfunction. They've never been told Jesus not only set them free from sin's penalty, but He's also set them free from sin's power. They don't have to live like a slave when God calls them His children. Yet Satan often convinces us we're still in a prison and we're still in chains, so when we could walk away, we stay.

It's known that in India, the way one trains an Indian elephant as a beast of burden begins when they are still in adolescence. The elephant trainer will chain the back leg of the young elephant to a stake. The young elephant will pull against the chain for days trying to get free. But after days and days of pulling and kicking, he realizes finally the chain is too strong and he gives up. He stops pulling against it. He stops fighting against it. He gives in to it. For the rest of that elephant's life, all the handler will have to do is tie a small rope around its leg, attach it to a stake, and the elephant will stay when he could easily walk away. He is now fully grown and unbelievably strong and powerful. The chain that used to hold him couldn't possibly hold him now, much less the tiny rope that is now tied around his leg. But he doesn't walk away because he's now been trained to stay. He's convinced the rope wrapped around his leg is stronger than the power inside of him. Do you understand that is the condition of many Christians?

It's time for some of us to stand up and walk away! You don't have to stay. You are free to flee! The only question is, "Who will you believe?" Your old master says,

"You're not free, you're still in captivity." Your new Master says, "You are free—I set you free at Calvary!" You will obey whoever you believe. Ephesians 2:8-9 says, "For by grace you have been saved through faith, and that not of yourselves; it is the gift of God, not of works, lest anyone should boast." We are set free from sin's power in exactly the same way we are set free from sin's penalty— by grace through faith. We need God's grace. Grace is God's work done on our behalf. And you appropriate God's grace through your faith—faith in what God says. That's how you appropriate all the promises of God in your life—by faith and not our works. We are unable to save or free ourselves. All of our works and pulling against the chains will end in futility and a life lived in captivity. It is for this very reason Jesus went to Calvary. It is His work alone that has set us free. That is our ultimate reality and true identity. That chain that used to bind you is now nothing more than a small rope around your leg. The liar has convinced you that you still have to stay, but Jesus has given you the power to walk away.

You are free to flee!

Do you see why Satan wants so desperately to cause you to doubt the truth of God's Word and the reality of

God's Son? He wants his lies to become a false reality for us all, which shapes our identity and eventually becomes our destiny. This is the condition of the vast majority of Christians. They have been caught in a false reality. They embraced a lie of the enemy and opened the door for Satan to redefine their identity. In the heat of temptation, whoever you believe is the one who will win the day. Regardless of what you feel, you must believe the truth. You may not feel free when you are about to click on pornography. You may not feel free when your body is screaming, "Get me that nicotine!" But the truth is you are FREE! Jesus set you free! And whoever you believe is who you will obey. You will serve whichever master you choose based on which one you believe.

CHAPTER 12

FREE TO FLEE

In the heat of temptation, remember it is Satan who tempts but God who tests. There are always two agendas—God's and Satan's. My former coaches used to say to us as they were about to run us into the ground, "Boys, today we're going to test your mettle." They intended to find out what we were made of, to test our strength and stamina. In the same way that fire tests metal and makes the metal stronger, God will allow the mettle of our faith to be tested in order to make our faith stronger and better than it would be if left untested. Metalsmiths know that fire makes the metal pliable. Only then is the metalsmith able to mold and fashion it into something usable and of value. God does the same thing in our lives in the fires of temptation. He is molding us and shaping us into something He can use. Fire removes the impurities from metal. Do you see why God allows us to be tempted? What Satan hopes to use to weaken us and eventually destroy us is the very thing God uses to strengthen and fortify us.

God makes a promise for us all:

> *No temptation has overtaken you except such as is common to man; but God is faithful, who will not allow you to be tempted beyond what you are able, but with the temptation will also make the way of escape, that you may be able to bear it.*
> —1 CORINTHIANS 10:13

Temptation is part of the human experience. Remember, even Jesus in His humanity was tempted. Temptation itself is not a sin, but we have to learn how to wage war against it or it will become a sin and then our prison. People often say, "Pastor Phil, I am caught in this sin, and I am just praying that God will take this temptation away from me, and I have pleaded and I have prayed but God will not hear me. He will not take away this temptation." To that, I usually respond by saying, "Well, be careful what you pray for. God could take temptation from you, but to do it He would have to kill you!" As long as we live in these fallen physical bodies, we will have to deal with temptation because our physical bodies are the seat of the sin nature that dwells within them (see James 1:13-14). When you are free from this body and in heaven in your glorified body, you will be free from temptation.

Until then, temptation is a part of the human experience of our fallen condition.

While you can never be free from temptation this side of heaven, you can be free from sin. First Corinthians 10:13 tells us God will not allow us to be tempted beyond what we are able to handle. And with that temptation God will make a way of escape. You can escape the temptation so you don't have to sin. What is the way of escape? God declares it in the very next verse: "Therefore, my beloved, flee from idolatry" (1 Cor. 10:14). You are free to flee. You don't have to stay—you have the power to walk away. You are no longer Satan's prisoner, and you are no longer sin's slave. The sin that feels like a chain around your leg is nothing more than a rope from which you can walk away. The only question left is, "Who will you believe?" Don't be like Eve who was deceived because of what she saw. Move instead according to what God has said.

God has said, "You are free to flee!" Flee from idolatry because all idolatry will lead us back into captivity. And while we've been set free at Calvary, Satan wants to lure us back into slavery—so *FLEE*!

One night, years ago, while on duty as a member of the KCPD, I pulled into a local convenience store well after midnight. As I was walking in, just "coincidentally," a couple of strippers were walking in as well. They had just gotten off work at the local "gentlemen's club" just up the street. They were beautiful—and they barely had anything on. We got to the door of the store at about the same time, and one of them looked directly at me and asked, "Do you ever cheat on your wife?" Then they started saying some other things that I am not about to put in print. I didn't know what to say, but I knew what to do. I got back to my car, and I drove away. I peeled out of there and made the "great escape." I chose the promise God made when He said He "will not allow you to be tempted beyond what you are able, but with the temptation will also make the way of escape" (1 Cor. 10:13). There is the escape. You leave! The longer you choose to stay, the less likely you are going to walk away. That was a moment where Satan was *tempting* but God was *testing*, and my faith got stronger.

I look over the course of my eight years on the PD, and I cannot tell you how many times something like that happened to me. The entire time there were two agendas—God's and Satan's. Satan was tracking me; he was trying to figure out my combination. God was "proving" me for the ministry while Satan was trying to disqualify me. I was a light for the Gospel in that police department. I was sharing my faith, and I was winning people to Christ. Because of that, he wanted to destroy my reputation, ruin my credibility, and blow up my family. He is trying to crack our combination every moment of every day. At the time my life intersected with the lives of these two beautiful and barely-clothed young ladies, I thought it was just coincidental. I've since learned that there are no coincidences. Satan was pulling the strings of these young ladies. He had sent them on a mission to which they were completely unaware. They were unwittingly on a mission from him—prisoners "unaware." He knew my past wounds and he knew the bait I might take. He knows yours too. He was trying to crack my combination just like he is trying to crack yours.

You don't fight temptation—
you flee from temptation.

It doesn't matter what form of temptation it might be. You still deal with it the same way—you don't fight it, you flee from it. It might be something far more subtle and much less sinister than infidelity or adultery. I must confess that while I have never had a love affair since the day I said "I do" with any woman other than my wife, I have struggled with an ongoing love "affair" with ice cream for many years. My wife loves bringing it home from every trip to the grocery store. I try to watch what I eat, but the ice cream seems to call my name! I tell my wife, "Darling you are being used of the devil. Stop bringing that ice cream home!" Here's the point—to the best of your ability, stop allowing temptation and opportunity to intersect. You can't always avoid temptation, but you can usually avoid opportunity. This is the meaning of Romans 13:14, which tells us to "make no provision for the flesh, to fulfill its lusts." Don't keep putting yourself in the position to cave into temptation.

Stop allowing temptation and opportunity to intersect.

I have learned there are certain people and places I need to distance myself from. At 21 years of age when I began following Jesus, leaving behind my life as the prodigal son far from God, I learned right away I needed to find a new playground and new playmates. There were people and places that posed a temptation for me, and they weren't good for me. What do you do? RUN! I do not know how many times people who are trying to break free from an adulterous relationship have sat in my office saying, "Phil, I think we can at least still be friends." That is like an alcoholic trying to quit drinking and getting a job in a liquor store or a crack cocaine addict trying to stop doing crack and hanging out at a crack house. Do not walk. Run! Flee from temptation as fast as you can. You are free to flee!

Paul says to flee from idolatry (see 1 Cor. 10:14). Take a moment to consider if you may have an idol in your life. It can be something as obvious as watching pornography or something much more subtle like watching too much television. It can be something as obvious as turning to nicotine to take a little stress off or something far more subtle like compulsive shopping or overeating. Anytime we turn to something other than God to find a source of security or strength or comfort, we are erecting an idol in our life. It can be just a secret place in your mind you go to occasionally to entertain a wicked thought or fantasy. You are building an idol, and guess what? It always will lead to captivity. That is why Paul says, "Flee from idolatry."

Eve was taken captive by idolatry. I am convinced the tree had become an idol to her. She was obsessed by it. She was absolutely fixated on it and mesmerized by it. There were thousands of trees from which she could eat and thousands of square miles through which she could roam. The Garden of Eden was a very large place. But Satan knew the exact day, the exact time she would be at that one tree because he had been tracking her, stalking her, and studying her. He knew exactly when she would be there. He was waiting to ambush her. He had watched her go back to that tree over and over again at the same time every day. He was ready that day when she went to the tree. The question is, "Eve, why did you stay? You could have walked away."

Satan knows your place of idolatry. He knows your tree of temptation, just as he does mine. And he is ready for you, and he is waiting when you go back to that tree. The question is this: Will you stay when you have the power to walk away? You are free to flee, but the longer you stay at the tree, the less chance you have to break

free. You do not fight temptation, you flee from temptation. When the Son has set you free, you are free to flee.

CHAPTER 13

OUR DELIVERANCE

And they overcame him by the blood of the Lamb and by the word of their testimony, and they did not love their lives to the death.

—REVELATION 12:11

On a recent trip to the Holy Land, as I stood on the ruins of the ancient city of Megiddo overlooking the plains of Armageddon, my thoughts turned to the story of the Exodus. Megiddo was one of the Canaanite cities taken by Joshua as the ancient Hebrews made conquest of the Promised Land. It was the city that guarded this fertile plain which the Bible tells us will become the location of the last battle shortly before Christ's Second Coming. It's little wonder why it was called, "the land that flows with milk and honey." The plain of Armageddon, also known as the Jezreel Valley, is a place of fertility, beauty, and bounty in a region of the world that is otherwise a dry and arid desert. All the ancient peoples wanted it, but it was the Jews to whom God promised it.

You know the story of the Exodus. It was my story for many years and perhaps yours as well. God miraculously delivered the Hebrew slaves from Egyptian tyranny, but when it came time to enter the Promised Land, they chose to stay in a different kind of captivity. They only went *halfway*. They had enough faith to get out of Egypt but not enough faith to enter into the Promised Land. Even though they had been delivered from bondage immediately, they spent 40 years in the wilderness. They had been set free, but they still lived like they were in captivity. They believed the lie of the enemy instead of crossing over to the land of liberty—a land that flowed with milk and honey. Ten of the twelve spies Moses sent to survey the land returned shaking in their boots with a report of doom and gloom: "The Canaanites are too big for us to beat in battle. They'll probably eat our children for breakfast!" They chose to stay instead of going all the way.

The tragic truth is an entire generation of liberated slaves lived and died in the wilderness, never once laying eyes on the beauty and bounty of all God had promised them. As Christians, that's who we are—liberated slaves.

Like the ancient Hebrews, many of us only go halfway as well. Satan prepares giants in our lives to keep us from crossing over into the joy of sweet deliverance. That is the sad story of far too many born-again, blood-bought children of God. Jesus delivered them from sin's penalty, but they live in bondage to sin's power. They live their entire lives halfway to their land of promise, stuck in a wilderness of mediocrity and only partial victory.

Remember: If God has promised it, He will perform it; but that which we already possess positionally, must be appropriated practically.

Possessing the Promised Land won't come easy, but you are guaranteed victory because of what Jesus did at Calvary.

Revelation 12:11 reveals the three ways our deliverance comes...

1. Through our divine declaration
    ➡ *by the blood of the Lamb*

2. Through our mouth's confession
    ➡ *the word of their testimony*

3. Through our heart's submission
    ➡ *they did not love their lives to the death*

BY THE BLOOD OF THE LAMB

Doctrinally, Revelation 12:11 is about the tribulation saints—the followers of Jesus in the coming seven-year tribulation who will refuse to follow the Antichrist and will instead follow the true and living Christ. The Antichrist, empowered and possessed by Satan, will make war with them to overcome them, but in the end they will overcome him!

While we aren't living in the tribulation, Satan wars against us with our own tribulation. In the same way the future saints of God will overcome Satan, we too can overcome his every attack. It begins with understanding our positional reality. Our position "in Adam" was different from our position "in Christ." When our fallen father Adam sinned, legal dominion was passed from Adam to Satan. All of Adam's children would be born alive physically but dead spiritually under sin's penalty and Satan's tyranny. Our legal position was that we were "in sin" before God and under Satan's dominion. By legal position, I mean that we had a legal debt before God we could not pay. And Satan, as the accuser and prosecutor, could make a legal claim against us.

> *But God, who is rich in mercy, because of His great love with which he loved us, even when we were dead in trespasses, made us alive together with Christ (by grace you have been saved), and raised us up together, and made us sit together in the heavenly places in Christ Jesus.*
> —EPHESIANS 2:4-6

The key to the above passage is the final three words: "in Christ Jesus." Because we are no longer "in sin," our legal position before God is now "in Christ." By divine declaration, we are now blameless, guiltless, sinless, and spotless. In the American criminal justice system, the accused stands before a judge and that judge declares their guilt or innocence. In the same way, God from the great tribunal room in heaven, has declared our innocence of all sin because Jesus took all our sin and placed it on Him (see 2 Cor. 5:21). We are innocent by divine declaration. The Judge has legally exonerated us from all our sin. We were born the first time "in sin," but we've been born again "in Him." We have been delivered from sin's penalty and Satan's tyranny through *the blood of the Lamb.* It's our positional reality and our true identity because of the legal transaction that took place at Calvary.

While we were in sin, Satan had legal rights over our lives. Now that we are in Christ, Satan has lost those rights. Jesus alone possesses the legal rights to our lives because *the blood of the Lamb* has legally purchased us out of slavery and pardoned us of sin's penalty. By divine declaration, legally before God...

- We are holy and sinless already "in Christ."

- We have power and authority already "in Christ."

- We are triumphant and victorious already "in Christ."

- We are seated in heavenly places already "in Christ."

- We have dominion over sin and Satan "in Christ."

As children of God, it is our ultimate reality and true identity. We have a new Father and a new family through what Jesus did at Calvary. The Apostle Paul made it clear when he wrote that "by grace you have been saved." It is all the work of Christ and not our work at all. Jesus announced this eternal truth on the cross when He declared, "It is finished." John confirmed it in the Book of Revelation as he looked through the lens of prophecy and saw how the tribulation saints "overcame him [Satan] by the blood of the Lamb." Paul expounded on this ultimate weapon in our spiritual armory in Ephesians 6:10-17, urging us three times to "stand." Stand on what? You stand on what God has said and what Jesus did...the finished work of Calvary.

If you're standing on any other ground, you're on shaky ground. No matter how religious or how righteous you may be, when you try to stand on your works, you have nothing at all on which to stand. As the Prophet Isaiah proclaimed in Isaiah 64:6, our works are nothing more than "filthy rags." Satan knows this. In fact, he's working around the clock to get you to stand on any other work other than Christ's.

BY THE WORD OF THEIR TESTIMONY

God made a covenant with Abraham, the father of the Hebrews, in Genesis 15:18-21. By divine declaration, God promised Abraham and his descendants a specific piece of real estate known as the Promised Land. It was God's promise to all the children of Abraham through Isaac and Jacob. From the moment God declared it, this land became the birthright of every Hebrew.

> *And if children, then heirs—heirs of God and joint heirs with Christ...*
>
> —ROMANS 8:17

As children of God and the spiritual children of Abraham (see Gal. 3:16), God has made a covenant promise with us as well. It's our "real estate" and our birthright. Please don't take this the wrong way and try to steal the promises God made to the Jews as some do. The Church is not the spiritual Israel, and as non-Jewish believers, God has not promised us a specific piece of real estate in the Middle East.

Our real estate and our birthright is a Promised Land spiritually beyond anything we can ask or think. It's the abundant life that Jesus declared He came to give to us in John 10:10—free from captivity and Satan's dominion. It's a fruitful life of beauty and bounty.

The Promised Land was bestowed upon the children of Israel by divine declaration, but they still had to take possession of it. In the same way your spiritual land of promise—life abundantly in Christ—is already yours, it's up to you to take possession of it. If you don't, you'll live no differently than the generation of Hebrews who were delivered out of Egyptian bondage but never entered into the life of abundance God had prepared for them.

Yes it's yours, but Satan will do everything in his power to keep you from ever experiencing it. You're going to have to wage war in the spirit—the same way the tribulation saints will overcome Satan: "By the word of your testimony."

You appropriate your God-given authority through the "blood of the Lamb." You exercise that authority by the "word of your testimony."

You have authority spiritually *by the blood of the Lamb*. Jesus said, "All authority has been given to Me in heaven and on earth" (Matt. 28:18). We are "in Christ," which means we have kingdom authority as "kings and priests" who will one day reign on the earth (see Rev. 5:10). We are no longer under Satan's dominion but rather he is under ours. First Corinthians 6:3 tells us that one day we will "judge [fallen] angels." While we were created a "little lower than the angels" (Heb. 2:7), we now have dominion over Satan and his angels—just as Adam had before he sinned. Jesus said, "Behold, I give you the authority to trample on serpents and scorpions, and over all the power of the enemy" (Luke 10:19). That means we don't have to obey Satan and his demonic host; they have to obey us!

Years ago as a member of the KCPD, I became a Field Training Officer (FTO) for rookie police officers who had just graduated from the police academy. Part of a new officer's training is to be assigned to an FTO for a three-month "break in" period. The job of an FTO is to train a new officer in real-life situations encountered on the streets rather than in the controlled environment of the academy. I quickly discovered some new officers had a difficult time asserting themselves and taking control of difficult situations. Even though they'd been given delegated civil authority, they would hang back and not use it. They were fearful and insecure. They'd been given a badge and a gun, but still they were reluctant to use the authority they'd been given. That is the condition of many a Christian. As a child of God you have been given a *badge* and a *gun*. You've been given spiritual authority in Christ and spiritual weapons so you can win. As a child of God, you are "armed and dangerous"! You may not know it, but Satan sees you as a threat to his kingdom. All he can do is hope you never learn how dangerous you are and how to exercise your authority over him.

Here's a simple analogy to help you understand this vital truth. If someone steps out into an intersection and sticks out his hand as if to tell me to stop, I'm going to drive around him and keep right on going. He doesn't have the authority to tell me to stop. On the other hand, if that person is wearing a uniform and a badge and holds up his hand for me to stop, it doesn't matter if the light is green, I'm going to stop. He has been given authority to take control of that intersection. However, if that same officer is just standing on the curb doing nothing, I'm going to keep driving. He has the authority to seize control of the intersection, but he's not exercising it.

As Christians, we have God's delegated authority. But some Christians either don't know it or won't exercise it. Perhaps they're too fearful to step out into the intersection of life and take control. There are just too many "giants." When you understand the power and authority you possess in Christ, all of that can change. Michael the Archangel understood the chain of command as he disputed with the devil over the body of Moses. Jude 9 records that he "dared not bring against him [Satan] a reviling accusation, but said, 'The Lord rebuke you!'" He knew in God's hierarchy of authority that Satan, even in his fallen condition, still outranked him. So he appealed to a higher name that outranked Satan. That name is the Lord—the name that is above every name (see Phil. 2:9).

Everything God does, He does through a chain of command. Adam was given dominion over the earth. He was high on the hierarchy, second only to God Himself. He was higher on the chain of command than even Satan who had fallen and been demoted by

God because of his rebellion. When Adam sinned, he was demoted and had no choice but to relinquish his dominion and give it back to Satan. Sin does the same thing in our own lives. It makes us once again subservient to Satan's dominion.

Your mouth is for confession.

If you confess with your mouth the Lord Jesus and believe in your heart that God has raised Him from the dead, you will be saved. For with the heart one believes unto righteousness, and with the mouth confession is made unto salvation.
—ROMANS 10:9-10

What we believe in our hearts is directly connected to what we confess with our mouths. Our confession is simply our profession of faith in God's divine declaration. When Jesus said, "For out of the abundance of the heart the mouth speaks" (Matt. 12:34), He was saying that our destiny is in our words. You appropriated God's promise of salvation by first believing in your heart what God had said and what Jesus did. Then you confessed with your mouth that Jesus is Lord. You appropriate all the other promises of God in exactly the same manner.

As you step out in faith to possess your Promised Land (that life God has promised you), you must believe what God has said with your heart and confess it with your mouth. That is the "word of your testimony." In the same way you were delivered from sin's penalty, you are delivered from sin's power.

Two made a confession of faith in what God had said. The others made a confession of faith in Satan's lies instead.

You can see this played out as the 12 spies Moses sent to spy out the Promised Land came back to give a report of the land to the rest of the camp. Joshua and Caleb came back and gave a report of the land saying in Numbers 13:30, "Let us go up at once and take possession, for we are well able to overcome it." The "word of their testimony" became their destiny. Of the 12 spies, only Joshua and Caleb would eventually cross over and possess the land. On the other hand, ten of the spies came back and gave a different report saying in verses 31-33, "We are not able to go up against the people, for they are stronger than we...the land through which we have gone as spies is a land that devours its inhabitants, and all the people whom we saw in it are men of great stature...and we were like grasshoppers in our own sight..." That was the "word of their testimony," and it sadly became their destiny as well. Unlike Joshua and Caleb, they would never possess the land; in fact, they died in the wilderness. What was the difference? God had promised the land to all of them, but only two of them would take possession of God's promises. The difference was that some believed and confessed it with their words, while most did not.

Now don't confuse what I'm saying with the ever popular "name it and claim it" theology that teaches if you have enough faith in what you are saying, God has to do it. How foolish! Who are we to think we can "claim" what God has never "named" as if God has to do it simply because we said it? God is under no mandate to perform that which He has never promised. On the other hand, whatever God has first "named," we can "claim." If God has promised it, He will perform it—but only if we first believe it and then confess it.

Do you need to be delivered from Satan's snare and the power of besetting sin? Repent of your sin and renounce Satan's right to rule your life. This is a process you will repeat many times in your life as you wage war with the enemy. Confession is how you put God's promises in motion. It's how you were delivered from sin's penalty and how you are delivered from Satan's tyranny.

Take inventory of your life and repent of your sin. Ask Jesus to reveal any unclean thing you may be harboring in your heart. Pray Psalm 139:23-24, "Search me,

O God, and know my heart; try me, and know my anxieties; and see if there is any wicked way in me..." And then begin praying First John 1:9, "If we confess our sins, He is faithful and just to forgive us our sins and to cleanse us from all unrighteousness." You must understand that sin puts us under Satan's dominion in the same way it did Adam. This is why you can be delivered from sin's penalty but still live under Satan's tyranny. You can be delivered "in Christ" positionally, but not practically and experientially. That's why some of us have never enjoyed life abundantly even though we've been delivered from hell eternally.

Our sin builds a covenant with Satan and ties our soul to a cruel master.

Nobody wakes up in the morning and thinks to themselves, "Today I'll form a pact with Satan and sell my soul to the devil." But that's what we do when we choose to sin in the same area again and again. Sin returns to Satan certain rights to our lives. This is why even when Jesus has set us free, we can go right back into captivity. Ephesians 4:27 says, don't "give place to the devil." Satan has lost his place in our lives "in Christ," but sin gives Satan back that place he lost. If you do not repent of that sin and instead keep repeating it, it will become a stronghold. Repent of your sin and take back that place in your life Satan has stolen. That's God's ground. It's His real estate. It belongs to Christ! Then verbally renounce Satan's right to rule your life another moment.

The strength of sin

is in its secrecy.

Confess your trespasses to one another, and pray for one another, that you may be healed.
—JAMES 5:16

Confession goes beyond just admitting your sins to God. There is something powerful that takes place when you confess your sins to others. I'm convinced this is why many Christians have been forgiven of their sin but haven't been healed from their sin. This was my condition for many years. I was forgiven but not healed. I only began finding healing when I came out of hiding. *Authenticity and transparency in true biblical community is essential for healing!* Authenticity and transparency breaks the strength of besetting sin, which is secrecy. Satan operates in the shadows, but never in the light. The Apostle John said it this way:

But if we walk in the light as He is in the light, we have fellowship with one another, and the blood of Jesus Christ His Son cleanses us from all sin.

—1 JOHN 1:7

You can't go solo. You need true Christian community in the body of Christ for this reason. Maybe it's a trusted and mature Christian friend or group of friends. Maybe it's a pastor or Christian counselor. Maybe it's your small group you meet with from church. You need people in your life to whom you can expose all the darkness and bring it into the light. You may confess your sin directly to Jesus and be forgiven, but confessing it to others is for your healing. The one gets you out of Egypt; the other ushers you into your Promised Land!

For I, the Lord your God, am a jealous God, visiting the iniquity of the fathers upon the children to the third and fourth generations of those who hate Me, but showing mercy to thousands, to those who love Me and keep My commandments.

—EXODUS 20:5-6

There is far more in these verses than any of us can probably begin to fathom, but first understand what it is not. It is not teaching that God holds children personally accountable for the sins of their fathers, grandfathers, and great-grandfathers. On the other hand, what it is teaching is that the sins of one's ancestors profoundly impact their descendants in the present. This is why you can easily see certain sins that seem to follow one's family tree. Sins like alcoholism, drug addiction, abuse, adultery, and sexual immorality seem to follow certain families from one generation to the next. Some of this, of course, is because of learned behavior on the part of children. Children will imitate their parents. But this verse is addressing more than kids passing on the bad behavior of their parents.

Repent and renounce generational sin.

Again, the spiritual realm works through a chain of command—spiritual channels of authority. Fathers represent authority in their families. The attack on fatherhood in our society is nothing less than Satan's all-out attack on the family that God instituted beginning in Genesis 2:18. Fathers represent a spiritual covering. The attempt to marginalize the role of men, and dads specifically, in our society is straight from the pit of hell. In many ways, dad is a family's destiny and Satan knows it. The curse on our land is directly tied to a fatherless rate in America of more than 40 percent. Satan knows if he can eliminate dad, he can wreak havoc on the family. He does it again and again, and his diabolical attack on fathers can affect a family for generations.

Suppose a father, who represents spiritual authority over his children, becomes an alcoholic, a porn addict, an adulterer, or an abuser who walks out on his children's mother. Even worse, what if he molests his own daughter or physically abuses his own sons. He has unwittingly entered into a covenant with Satan because of his sin. In so doing, he has given dominion of his family over to Satan in the same way our father Adam sold all of his sons and daughters into slavery and under Satan's authority. That's why generation after generation, another father passes on the dysfunction to his own son as it had been passed on to him. It's more than a learned behavior and it's more than dysfunction—it's demonic. It's a satanic spirit that was given rights over a family that is passed from one generation to the next.

How do you break that generational curse? *You repent and renounce it!* You repent of that family sin and renounce Satan's right to rule your family any longer. You can be the one to begin a brand-new family tree—a spiritual family tree that enjoys the blessing of God for generations to come. Consider God's promise in the last part of Exodus 20:6: "But showing mercy to thousands, to those who love Me and keep My commandments." Your decision to believe and obey God will bring blessing on your family and to thousands you will never even meet for generations to come. Put Satan on notice. Confess Jesus as Lord. Finally, follow the example of those tribulation martyrs who...

DID NOT LOVE THEIR LIVES TO THE DEATH

What does this mean? It means the tribulation saints will choose death over life. It means their ultimate victory will be found not in their lives, but in their deaths. They will choose to lay down their lives and overcome the devil with their own death. They will choose Jesus over their very lives. Instead of loving and trying to preserve their lives, they will let go of and lose their lives. What looks outwardly like a great victory for the enemy is actually his defeat. You can't defeat an enemy who's not afraid to die because they have nothing left to lose. This is our ultimate victory over our enemy. When we let go of our lives and die to our flesh, we have nothing left to lose.

 In losing it all, we gain it all!

Whoever desires to come after Me, let him deny himself, and take up his cross, and follow Me. For whoever desires to save his life will lose it, but whoever loses his life for My sake and the gospel's will save it.

—Mark 8:34-35

While untold millions of followers of Jesus in the last 2000 years of Church history have literally laid down their lives for Christ, there is another way the rest of us can lay down our own lives. While we should be prepared to die for Christ, what it really means is to live for Christ.

> *I have been crucified with Christ; it is no longer I who live, but Christ lives in me; and the life which I now live in the flesh I live by faith in the Son of God, who loved me and gave Himself for me.*
>
> —GALATIANS 2:20

To deliver us from sin's penalty, Christ died. To be delivered from sin's power, you must die.

It's the cross that strikes the fatal blow to Satan. It's the cross that has crushed the head of the serpent (see Gen. 3:15). Two thousand years ago, God saw us "in Christ," which means the cross on which Christ died is the same cross on which we died as well. It happened once already in history, but now we must do it daily.

Paul said in First Corinthians 15:31, "I die daily." We died positionally "in Christ" already, but now we must die daily to possess our Promised Land experientially. On a practical level, this means coming to a place of unconditional surrender to the Lordship of Jesus Christ. Practically speaking, this is what it means when Revelation 12:11 says, "They did not love their lives to the death."

Our hearts are for submission.

We are set free from Satan's tyranny and promised abundant life by divine declaration. We then begin taking possession by our mouth's confession, and most importantly, our heart's submission. Remember, as mortals it's mandated that we live under a spiritual master. It will either be Christ or it will be Satan. We are under a spiritual chain of command, and we will live under the power of our choosing. Jesus taught no one can serve two masters, but you get to choose yours. You can believe and obey Jesus and enter into covenant with Him, or you can believe and obey Satan and enter into a covenant with him. When we live under Satan's authority, it will always bring a life of captivity and slavery. But when we submit to Christ's authority, He promises a life lived abundantly and with liberty. This is the ultimate deliverance from the power of sin and Satan.

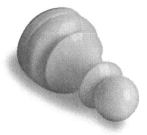

You cannot live with liberty apart from submitting to Christ's authority.

Jesus announced in Luke 4:18 that He came "to proclaim liberty to the captives." He can make that bold proclamation to bring about our freedom and liberty from Satan's authority and tyranny because He is the one with all power and authority. Liberty and authority are two sides of the same coin. To the degree you submit to Christ's authority is the degree you will live with His promise of liberty. Only as you begin living completely in obedience, will you start living truly abundantly in your Promised Land spiritually. Most attempts at changing the self-destructive or sinful patterns in our lives are nothing more than self-reformation and behavior modification. What we truly need is inner transformation—a transformation of our heart condition. More often people attempt to overcome sin and temptation by way of suppression. They try to suppress their sin and suppress the temptation. They might succeed for a while, but eventually their "self-will" kicks in and they will cave in again. Suppression is like trying to just mow over the weeds in your yard to get rid of them. Unless you deal with the root of the problem, they will always come back again.

This is what Jesus meant when He said to "take up your cross daily" and follow Him (Luke 9:23). In Jesus' day, a cross was not something you wore, it was something you bore. You carried it to your own execution. It was not something of beauty—it was something that was brutal, bloody, and ugly. His teaching is clear. The way to a life of transformation comes only by way of the crucifixion. The cross strikes the fatal blow to all the power of Satan. You can live in the Promised Land, but only if you're willing to die—and die daily. "In Christ" you died once already (see Gal. 2:20), but now you must do it daily (see 1 Cor. 15:31) to live it out experientially.

The way to overcome is not by a life of suppression but a life of submission.

God resists the proud, but gives grace to the humble. Therefore submit to God. Resist the devil and he will flee from you. Draw near to God and He will draw near to you. Cleanse your hands, you sinners; and purify your hearts, you double minded. Lament and mourn and weep! Let your laughter be turned to mourning and your joy to gloom. Humble yourselves in the sight of the Lord, and He will lift you up.

—James 4:6-10

Only through crucifixion
can you live in the joy
of the resurrection.

Do you see the process to resist and overcome the devil? Humility brings submission to Christ's authority which sets us free from Satan's tyranny. Continually repent of sin and submit to Jesus' right to rule your life. This is how you resist the devil. Satan will flee from you because now you are a danger to his kingdom. Surrender all rights to Him, and you will find it impossible to surrender to sin. I've heard it said that He alone has the right to rule your life and His rule in your life is always right. Amen.

It was December 1989. My life had been that of the "prodigal son" in the "far country" (see Luke 15). Looking back, it's amazing to consider how much sin I'd managed to fit into my 21 years. I had been running from God and wrestling with God for a very long time. My life was full of sin, but I refused to give up and I refused to give in. I had been raised in a Christian family by very godly parents. I knew the Gospel and knew the difference between right and wrong. Yet I had chosen a lot of things that were wrong even though I knew what was right. I had prayed to receive Christ as my Savior as a six-year-old little boy one Sunday night at church. Driving home that day for winter break, all that seemed like a long time ago and a long way away. I honestly no longer knew if I was even a Christian. I never doubted the truth. I never doubted who Jesus was. I never doubted He died and rose again. I knew there was a hell, and I knew there was a heaven. I knew there was a God, but I had lived my life like there wasn't. I had been Satan's prisoner, and though I had tried to break free, his hold on my life just seemed to grow stronger. I had tried and failed repeatedly.

As I drove home from Lawrence, Kansas for Christmas break, it had been lightly snowing. I was on the inside lane of the interstate when an 18-wheeler drifted over into my lane. I moved over on the narrow shoulder as far as I could when my tires caught the snow. The tracks in the snow told the story. I spun out of control, crossing over the median into the oncoming traffic— and then back over the median into the same lanes of traffic in which I had originally been traveling. It was just like you hear people say when facing a life and death situation—my life was "flashing before my eyes." What took only seconds seemed to be happening in slow motion. I saw another 18-wheeler approaching, and I knew we were going to collide. I resigned at that moment that I was doing to die. I still remember thinking right before impact: "I don't know where I'm going, but I guess I'm going to know now."

Clearly, I lived. Miraculously, I wasn't even harmed. But that is also the day I died. Though I lived, I died on that snowy December day in 1989. I went to a funeral that day, and my life was forever changed. The funeral I attended was mine. I went home, walked into my bedroom, and closed the door. I got down on my face before God and repented of my sin. I renounced Satan's right to rule my life and gave all rights to my life to the Lord Jesus Christ. I died to myself that day on my bedroom floor. When I got up, a resurrection had taken place and a new man lived. That day, the cross of Christ struck a fatal blow to the power of sin and Satan in my life. Every day since I have walked in the joy of the resurrection because I first chose the crucifixion. The Promised Land is yours already by divine declaration. But you take possession by way of crucifixion.

And they overcame him by the blood of the Lamb and by the word of their testimony, and they did not love their lives to the death.
—REVELATION 12:11

Today is a good day for you to die. Until you've fully died, you will never be fully alive. Satan, you lose.

ABOUT PHIL HOPPER

Phil Hopper has been the Lead Pastor of Abundant Life Church in Lee's Summit, Missouri, since 2000. He watched God do extraordinary things in the life of the church as it has grown from 100 people to a mega-church touching thousands and thousands of people each week. Prior to entering the ministry, he was a police officer and sergeant with the Kansas City Police Department where he served as a SWAT team member. It was through this experience that God uniquely prepared him for the ministry. Phil lives in the Lee's Summit area with his wife, Christa. They have three children: Jake, Makay, and Josh.

Printed in Great Britain
by Amazon